The fifth annual of
European editorial, book,
poster, advertising,
unpublished work, film
animation and design art.

Cinquième annuaire
européen d'illustration
de presse, du livre,
d'affiche, de publicité,
d'oeuvres non publiées,
du film d'animation et
du design.

Der fünfte Band des
Jahrbuches 'European
Illustration'–des Buches
über die Illustration auf
redaktionellem Gebiet,
im Buch, in Plakat und
Poster, in der Werbung,
in den unveröffentlichten
Arbeiten, im Trickfilm
und in der Gebrauchs-
graphik.

**European Illustration
1978/79**
Edited by
Edité par
Herausgegeben von
Edward Booth-Clibborn

Book designed by
Maquettiste du livre
Buch gestaltet von
David Pelham, London

Exhibition of original
artwork in this book
L'exposition d'oeuvres
d'art originales de ce livre
Die Ausstellung der
Originalarbeiten in
diesem Buch
ICA, The Mall, London
12.9.78–29.9.78

The captions and art-
work in this book have
been supplied by the
entrants. Whilst every
effort has been made to
ensure accuracy,
European Illustration
do not, under any cir-
cumstances, accept
responsibility for errors
or omissions.

Les légendes et oeuvres
d'art figurant dans ce
livre ont été fournies par
les personnes inscrites.
Bien que tout ait été fait
pour en assurer l'exacti-
tude, en aucun cas
European Illustration
n'accepte de respon-
sabilité en cas d'erreurs
ou d'omissions.

Die textlichen Angaben
zu den Abbildungen und
die Vorlagen dazu wurden
uns von den Einsendern
zur Verfügung gestellt.
Der genauen Wiedergabe
wurde grösste Sorgfalt
gewidmet; European
Illustration kann jedoch
unter keinen Umständen
die Verantwortung für
Fehler oder Auslassungen
übernehmen.

If you are an illustrator
working in Europe,
whose work has been
commissioned anywhere
in the world, you may
submit your work to the
1979 jury.

Etes vous un illustrateur
travaillant en Europe et
ayant reçu commande
d'oeuvres, n'importe où
dans le monde. Vous
pouvez alors soumettre
votre travail au jury en
1979.

Wenn Sie ein Illustrator
sind, der in Europe tätig
ist, und einem Auftrag
für eine Arbeit irgendwo
auf der Welt erhalten
haben, können Sie Ihr
Werk der Jury für 1979
unterbreiten.

European Illustration
12 Carlton House Terrace
London SW1Y 5AH
1978

Distribution/Auslieferung
All enquiries to:

European Illustration
12 Carlton House Terrace
London SW1Y 5AH.
01-839 2964

Printed in Italy by Arnoldo
Mondadori Editore.
Filmset by
Filmcomposition, London
Published by Polygon
Publishing Limited, Zurich.
Copyright ©1978

Contents
Table des Matières
Inhalt

At a time when the concept of a European identity is beginning to spread beyond political objectives over all aspects of daily life, presenting European Illustration '77'78 at the Georges Pompidou Centre was a fascinating experience for us. The exhibition, which attracted a wide public as well as professionals, was also an excellent opportunity to compare the experiences and achievements of illustration in countries interested in getting to know, understand and work with each other.

The illustrations in the exhibition, whether designed for posters and advertising campaigns, packaging, books, magazines or newspapers could appeal to visitors on two levels. Depending on people's nationality, the artwork was either comfortingly familiar to them, or quite new, in which case they were obliged to interpret the message. The understanding of this message requires a new concept of viewing, a quicker perception of meaning, as it is based on an essential immediate and ephemeral impact.

The items in this exhibition and the accompanying publication created an artificial and slightly deceptive view of illustration, since the work was seen out of context. Nonetheless the show was instructive for its demonstration of the variety of answers to the problem of passing on information visually, and for the imagination and technical mastery of the illustrators. It revealed the infinitely diverse needs of communication exigent in modern life, as well as the different levels of perception required to appeal to public regard. A comparison of work from several countries showing the client's wishes, the author's talent and the final realization of the illustration showed how widely different means of expression can be.

Illustration is, by its very nature, subject to demand and consequently loses some of the spontaneity and freedom which are the prerequisites of creative art. The wide scope given to illustrators by art directors is a happy concession to such restriction and the breadth of expression they enjoy can contribute greatly to public awareness of media art.

Lack of examples from certain countries and illustrators made the exhibition insufficiently representative in some cases. But European Illustration is more than a presentation of original artwork. With the addition of roughs showing the different stages of art direction and a reconstruction of Gabriel Pascalini's studio, the exhibition showed creation and work methods and the many interests involved in the world of illustration. Its success in Paris, as in other European capitals, is encouraging for the future. Meanwhile, it offered both French and foreign visitors to the Centre Pompidou a fresh insight into the special contribution of illustration to our daily life.

Au moment où l'idée européenne cherche à prendre racine, où elle déborde de l'objectif politique pour couvrir peu à peu tous les aspects et les moments de la vie quotidienne, présenter l'Illustration Européenne '77'78 au Centre Georges Pompidou à l'intention de son vaste public autant que des spécialistes de la communication sociale constituait pour nous une chance et une occasion passionnante, celles de confronter les expériences et les réussites de l'illustration dans des pays désormais décidés à se connaître, à se comprendre, à travailler ensemble.

L'illustration dans son ensemble, qu'elle s'applique aux affiches et aux campagnes publicitaires, aux emballages, aux couvertures de livres ou de magazines, aux emplacements dans les quotidiens a sollicité les visiteurs et les a replongé, suivant leur nationalité, dans un "déjà vu" sécurisant ou dans une nouveauté dont ils u'efforcaient de percer le message. La compréhension de ce message nécessite un nouvel apprentissage du regard, une perception de plus en plus rapide de sa signification. Son support est, par vocation, éphémère, autant que sa rencontre occasionnelle est souvent dispersée.

Le regroupement que constitue une telle exposition, la publication qui l'accompagne, apportent de ce fait une vision artificielle, un peu irréelle à l'illustration. Mais elle enrichit la connaissance par l'affirmation de la polymorphie dans les solutions, de l'imagination et de la maîtrise technique manifestées par tous les illustrateurs. Elle dévoile l'infinie diversité des besoins de communication exigés par la vie moderne autant que des multiples approches pour accéder à la sensibilité du public. Confronter entre plusieurs pays le désir client, la talent de l'auteur et l'accueil de la cible au message recherché, c'est montrer la multiplication à l'infini des expressions possibles ou nécessaires lorsqu'il s'agit de répondre aux besoins économiques, sociaux et culturels du plus grand nombre.

L'illustration est, par nature, soumise à la commande et perd de ce fait un peu de la spontanéité et de la liberté propres à l'oeuvre artistique. La confiance parfois accordée aux illustrateurs par les directeurs artistiques constitue un heureux palliatif à cette contrainte. Elle peut largement contribuer à la sensibilisation voire à l'éducation des arts plastiques par un contact quotidien avec la palette des couleurs et la diversité des formes.

L'exposition sur l'Illustration Européenne est allée au delà d'une présentation des oeuvres, des messages, des supports. Sur ce point d'ailleurs, une participation encore insuffisante de certains pays et illustrateurs ne lui donnait pas encore, au gré de certains, un caractère suffisamment représentatif. Sa réussite à Paris comme dans d'autres capitales européennes, est un encouragement pour l'avenir. Mais elle a montré par l'adjonction de documents de travail, d'interviews, par la reconstitution de l'atelier de conception de Gabriel Pascalini, les cheminements de la création, les méthodes de travail, la multiplicité des intérêts concernés par l'illustration, les beautés et les servitudes du métier. A ce titre, elle a permis aux visiteurs français et étrangers du Centre Pompidou de porter un regard nouveau sur l'environnement quotidien auquel participe et contribue l'illustration.

Zu einer Zeit, wo sich das Konzept einer europäischen Identität langsam über politische Objektiven hinaus auf alle Aspekte des täglichen Lebens ausbreitet, war es für uns eine faszinierende Aufgabe, European Illustration '77'78 im Georges Pompidou Zentrum zu Präsentieren. Die Ausstellung, die sowohl ein breites Publikum als auch Fachleute anzieht, bot darüberhinaus eine hervorragende Gelegenheit, Vergleiche anzustellen unter den Erfahrungen und Fortschritten der Illustration in Ländern, die daran interessiert sind, sich kennen und verstehen zu lernen und miteinander zu arbeiten.

Die Illustrationen der Ausstellung, ob für Poster und Werbekampagnen, Verpackung, Bücher, Zeitschriften oder Zeitungen konnten auf zwei Ebenen Anklang finden. Abhängig von der Nationalität des Besuchers waren ihm die Reinzeichnungen entweder wohl vertraut oder ganz neu, was wiederum bedeutete, dass die Aussage interpretiert werden musste. Das Begreifen dieser Aussage verlangt ein neues Konzept des Beschauens, ein schnelleres Wahrnehmungsvermögen, das im Wesentlichen auf dem sofortigen und flüchtigen Eindruck basiert.

Die Arbeiten dieser Ausstellung und des begleitenden Jahrbuchs bilden einen unechten und etwas trügerischen Überblick über die Illustration, da sie ohne Zusammenhang gesehen wird. Dennoch ist die Ausstellung lehrreich durch die Darstellung der vielfältigen Antworten zum Problem der visuellen Informationsweitergabe, und durch den Einfallsreichtum und die technische Überlegenheit der Illustratoren. Sie offenbart die unendlich verschiedenen Nöte der Kommunikation, so dringlich im modernen Leben, und die verschiedenen Ebenen der Wahrnehmung, die zur Anziehung eines Publikums notwendig sind. Ein Vergleich unter den Arbeiten aus verschiedenen Ländern, unter Berücksichtigung der Wünsche des Auftraggebers, des Talents des Autoren und die endgültige Realisation der Illustration zeigt, wie vielfältig die Art der Aussage sein kann.

Naturgemäss ist die Illustration dem Gesetz der Nachfrage unterworfen und verliert demzufolge an Ungezwungenheit und Freiheit – den Vorbedingungen der Kreativität. Das Ausmass an Bewegungsfreiheit, das den Illustratoren von Art Direktoren gewährt wird, ist eine glückliche Konzession, und die Breite der heute zu geniessenden Expression kann weitläufig zur öffentlichen Wahrnehmung der Medienkunst beitragen.

Durch Mangel an Einsendungen aus bestimmten Ländern war die Ausstellung teilweise nicht repräsentativ genug. Aber European Illustration ist mehr als eine Ausstellung von Reinzeichnungen. Durch Einbeziehung von Rohskizzen der verschiedenen Stadien der Art Direktion und die Rekonstruktion des Gabriel Pascalini Studios zeigte die Ausstellung Gestaltung und Arbeitsmethoden und die vielen Aspekte der Welt der Illustration.

Ihr Erfolg in Paris und anderen europäischen Städten ist ermutigen für die Zukunft. Den französischen und ausländischen Besuchern des Pompidou Zentrums verschaffte sie einen frischen Einblick in den Beitrag, den die Illustration in unserem täglichen Leben leisten kann.

Foreword
Jacques Mullender
Directeur du Centre de
Creation Industrielle
Centre Georges
Pompidou, Paris

This is the fifth annual of European media art, covering the areas of editorial, book, advertising, poster, design, unpublished work and film animation.

The jury looked at over 4,000 items from different European countries and selected 350, which are reproduced in this book. Looking at the work this year, you will see a general increase in freer style, well drawn illustration and a move away from airbrush and graphic style work. It is sad that the work that reaches us from Eastern Europe is still rather unimaginative. Perhaps it is the lack of competition and comparison which prevents illustrators working in Eastern Europe from achieving a higher standard of work.

The original art was first seen at the exhibition in London, which opened on September 12th 1978 at 12 Carlton House Terrace, before it travelled around Europe. We want to make sure that the show reaches as wide a European audience as possible, and we do need sponsors for this.

Last year, the exhibition had its première opening at the Georges Pompidou Centre in Paris to wide critical acclaim, as Le Monde said, 'European Illustration bears witness to the renewal of interest in illustration, which expresses forcefully the spirit of our time.' You will also read about the exhibition in our foreword, written by Jacques Mullender, Director of the C.C.I. at the Georges Pompidou Centre.

I would like to thank the jury of Cherriwyn Magill, Massin, Dick de Moei, Michael Rand, Helmut Rottke, Jacques Seguela and Alan Waldie for all their efforts. We have published their curricula vitae, since we feel that it is important for your to know their background, because jury members are selected for their professional ability to commission outstanding illustration.

We have included an index of the names and addresses of the illustrators, advertising agencies, design groups and publishers who have contributed to this annual and also the names of those illustrators who have contributed in the past.

Do write to me for further information or if you wish to submit work to next year's book and exhibition, or telephone on 01-839 2464.

Voici le cinquième album d'art européen des media, couvrant les domaines des magazines et journaux, de la publicité, des affiches, du design, des oeuvres non publiées et du film d'animation.

Le jury a examiné plus de 4,000 pièces de différents pays européens et en a chosi 350, qui se trouvent reproduites dans ce livre. Un examen du travail de l'année vous fera découvrir le progrès général d'un style plus libre, de l'illustration bien dessinée, et le retrait du style graphique et de l'aérographe. Il est triste de constater que les pièces qui nous viennent de l'Europe de l'Est sont pauvres en imagination. Peut-être est-ce le manque de concurrence et de comparaison qui empêche les illustrateurs travaillant en Europe de L'est d'atteindre un niveau de travail plus élevé.

Le travail original a été montré d'abord à Londres, à l'exposition inaugurée le 12 septembre 1978 à 12 Carlton House Terrace, avant de circuler en Europe. Nous voulons être sûrs que l'exposition atteigne le public européen le plus étendu, et nous recherchons des promoteurs à cette fin.

L'année dernière l'inauguration de l'exposition avait eu lieu au Centre Georges Pompidou à Paris et elle avait été reçue avec enthousiasme par la critique, à en juger par ce que disait Le Monde 'L'Illustration Européenne témoigne du renouvellement d'intérêt pour l'illustration qui exprime avec force l'esprit de notre temps.' Vous trouverez des informations sur l'exposition également dans notre avant-propos par Jacques Mullender, Directeur de C.C.I., du Centre Georges Pompidou.

Je tiens à remercier le jury composé de Cherriwyn Magill, Massin, Dick de Moei, Michael Rand, Helmut Rottke, Jacques Seguela et Alan Waldie de tous leurs efforts. Nous publions leur curriculum vitae car nous estimons qu'il est important que vous les connaissiez. Les membres du jury sont choisis en fonction de leur capacité professionnelle à commander de l'illustration exceptionnelle.

Nous avons inclu un index des noms et adresses des illustrateurs, agences publicitaires, groupes de designers et éditeurs qui ont contribué à cet album et aussi les noms des illustrateurs qui ont contribué les années précédentes.

Ecrivez-nous pour plus de renseignements, ou bien si vous voulez présenter votre travail pour le prochain album, ou téléphonez-nous 01-839 2464.

Dies ist das fünfte Jahrbuch der europäischen Medienkunst, das die Bereiche Redaktion, Bücher, Werbung, Poster, Gebrauchsgraphik, unveröffentlichte Arbeiten und Trickfilm umfasst.

Aus über 4,000 Arbeiten aus vielen europäischen Ländern wählte die Jury 350 aus, die in diesem Buch erscheinen. Ein Überblick über die diesjährigen Arbeiten zeigt einen zunehmend freieren Stil, gut ausgeführte Illustration und einen Trend weg von Spritztechnik und grafischem Arbeitsstil. Es ist bedauerlich, dass die aus Osteuropa eingesandten Arbeiten noch immer wenig Einfallsreichtum zeigen, was vielleicht dadurch zu erklären ist, dass Mangel an Wettbewerb und Vergleichsmöglichkeiten diese Illustratoren davon abhält, einen höheren Arbeitsstandard zu erreichen.

Die Originalarbeiten wurden in einer Ausstellung in London gezeigt, die am 12. September 1978 in 12 Carlton House Terrace begann und danach durch Europa reiste. Unser Ziel ist, die Arbeiten in möglichst breiten Teilen Europas auszustellen, aber dafür brauchen wir Unterstützung.

Im vorigen Jahr fand die Eröffnung der Ausstellung mit weitreichenden, positiven Kritiken im Georges Pompidou Zentrum in Paris statt. Le Monde kommentierte 'European Illustration ist Zeuge eines erneuten Interesses an der Illustration, die unseren Zeitgeist so eindrucksvoll zum Ausdruck bring.' Ein weiterer Kommentar über Ausstellung ist in einem Vorwort von Jacques Mullender enthalten, dessen Abteilung C.C.I. die Ausstellung im Georges Pomidou Zentrum arrangierte.

Für die Bemuhungen unserer Jury–Cherriwyn Magill, Massin, Dick de Moei, Michael Rand, Helmut Rottke, Jacques Seguela und Alan Waldie–möchte ich mich bedanken. Wir veröffentlichen Details ihrer Arbeitslaufbahnen, denn wir halten es für wichtig, ihren Hintergrund zu kennen, da die Mitglieder der Jury aufgrund ihrer beruflichen Fähigkeiten, hervorragende Illustrationen in Auftrag zu geben, ausgewählt werden.

Das Buch enthält einen Index der Namen und Adressen der Illustratoren, Werbeagenturen, Design-Gruppen und Verleger, die in diesem Jahr einen Beitrag geleistet haben, sowie die Namen der Illustratoren, deren Arbeiten in vergangenen Jahren gezeigt wurden.

Falls Sie an weiteren Einzelheiten interessiert sind oder Arbeiten für das nächstjahrige Buch und die Ausstellung einreichen möchten, bitte schreiben Sie oder rufen Sie mich unter 01-839 2464 an.

Introduction
Edward Booth-Clibborn
Chairman, Designers and
Art Directors' Association
London

Cherriwyn Magill
Art Director Macmillan Publishing Limited

Cherriwyn Magill is responsible for commissioning book jackets for two imprints. Macmillan London is the trade imprint with Fiction, Biography and Memoirs on its list. The other imprint is Macmillan Press, which is an academic list, and covers such subjects as Politics, Economics, Literature, History, Philosophy and Sociology.

Cherriwyn Magill est la responsable de commandes de jaquettes de livres pour deux noms. Macmillan London est le nom commercial pour la fiction, la biographie et les mémoires de leur liste. L'autre nom est Macmillan Press, qui est une liste académique, et comprend les sujets suivants: Politique, Economie, Littérature, Histoire, Philosophie et Sociologie.

Cherriwyn Magill ist verantwortlich für die Auftragserteilung von Buchumschlägen dür zwei Verlagszweige. Macmillan London ist der Fachzweig für Romane, Biografien und Memoiren, während der andere Zweig, Macmillan Press, akademische Themen wie Politik, Wirtschaft, Literatur, Geschichte, Philosophie und Soziologie umfasst.

Massin
Art Director Gallimard

Massin started his publishing career in book clubs. Through his wide experience of the profession, he has been responsible for the typographical interpretation of many famous books. He has also compiled and written 'Letter and Image' a book about the figuration of the latin alphabet from the Middle Ages to the present day. His next book, which will be published in the autumn, concerns the history of street cries from the Middle Ages to the time of Proust.
He has been the art director of Gallimard since 1961 and has been responsible for a great number of book covers, in particular for the Folio collection for which he has now commissioned over 1,000 covers.

Massin a commencé sa carrière publicitaire dans les Clubs de Livres.
Grace à sa vaste expérience de la profession, il a été responsable de l'interpretation typographique de nombreux livres. Il a également composé et écrit un livre 'Lettre et Image' sur la figuration dans l'alphabet latin du Moyen-âge à nos jours. Son prochain livre sera publié à l'automne et concerne l'histoire des cris de la ville depuis le Moyen-âge jusqu'aux temps de Proust.
Il a été Directeur artistique chez Gallimard depuis 1961 et a été responsable d'un grand nombre de jaquettes de livres, en particulier celles de la collection Folio qui compte maintenant plus de 1,000 couvertures.

Massin begann seine Verlagskarriere in Buchklubs. Im Laufe seiner langen Berufserfahrung war er verantwortlich für die typografische Interpretation vieler berühmter Bücher. Das von ihm geschriebene und zusammengestellte Buch 'Letter and Image' behandelt die bildliche Darstellung des lateinischen Alphabets vom Mittelalter bis zur Gegenwart. Sein nächstes Buch, das sich mit der Geschichte von Strassenausrufen vom Mittelalter bis zur Zeit Prousts beschäftigt, wird im Herbst erscheinen.
Seit 1961 ist er Art Direktor bei Gallimard und ist verantwortlich für zahlreiche Buchumschläge, insbesondere die der Folio Collection, für die er bereits mehr als 1,000 Umschläge in Auftrag gegeben hat.

Dick de Moei
Art Director Avenue Magazine & Zero Magazine

Dick de Moei studied at the Rijksacademie voor Beeldende Kunsten in Rotterdam
Between 1965 and 1970, he worked as a graphic designer for advertising and also as a visual account executive for Elcoma-Philips, Eindhoven.
In 1970 he became Art Director of Avenue Magazine and has since won many awards for art direction, including Silver Awards and Merit Awards from The Art Directors Club New York, the Dr Erich Salomon Prize and the 1st Prize from The Art Directors Club of the Netherlands.
He also teaches magazine design at the Tijdschriftpers foundation in The Netherlands.

Dick de Moei a étudié à la Rijksacademie voor Beeldende Kunsten à Rotterdam.
Entre 1965 et 1970, il a travaillé comme designer graphique de publicité et aussi comme Chef de Publicité pour Elcoma-Philips, Eindhoven.
En 1970 il est devenu Directeur artistique de Avenue Magazine et a depuis reçu de nombreux prix pour sa direction artistique, y compris: des prix d'argent et des prix de mérite du Art Directors Club New York, le Prix Dr. Erich Salomon et le 1er Prix du Club des Directeurs artistiques des Pays-Bas.
Il enseigne également le design de revue à la fondation Tijdschriftpers dans les Pays Bas.

Dick de Moei studierte an der Rijksacademie voor Beeldende Kunsten in Rotterdam.
Zwischen 1965 und 1970 arbeitete er als Grafiker in der Werbebranche und als Visual Account Executive für Elcoma-Philips in Eindhoven.
1970 wurde er Art Direktor des Avenue Magazine und hat seitdem etliche Auszeichnungen für Art Direktion gewonnen, u.a. Silber- und Verdienstpreise des Art Directors Club New York, den Dr. Erich Salomon Preis und den 1. Preis des Art Directors Club der Niederlande.
Er lehrt ausserdem Zeitschriftdesign an der Tijschriftpers Foundation in den Niederlanden.

Michael Rand
Art Director/Managing Editor
The Sunday Times Magazine

Michael Rand studied at Goldsmiths College of Art.
He worked as a freelance designer before joining
Beaverbrook Newspapers as consultant designer to
the Daily Express, where he pioneered the use of
diagrams and charts illustrating the daily news in
graphic form.
In 1963 he became Art Editor of the Sunday Times
Magazine. He then for a short time became Design
Director and Associate Editor of the Sunday Times.
However, he returned to the Sunday Times Magazine
as Art Director and Managing Editor.
He has won many awards for art direction, including
D&AD Silver and Gold Awards.

Michael Rand a fait ses études au Goldsmiths
College of Art.
Il a travaillé comme designer indépendant avant
d'entrer aux Beaverbrook Newspapers comme
designer conseiller au Daily Express, où il a mis en
oeuvre l'utilisation de diagrammes et de tableaux
pour illustrer les actualités quotidiennes sous
forme graphique.
En 1963 il est devenu Directeur artistique du Sunday
Times Magazine. Pendant quelque temps il est
devenu Directeur de Design et Rédacteur en-Chef
Adjoint du Sunday Times. Toutefois, il est retourné
au Sunday Times Magazine comme Directeur
artistique et Rédacteur.
Il a reçu de nombreux prix pour sa direction
artistique, y compris les prix d'or et d'argent du
D&AD.

Michael Rand studierte am Goldsmiths College of Art.
Er arbeitete als freiberuflicher Designer und wurde
dann beratender Designer der Daily Express
innerhalb der Beaverbrook Zeitungsgruppe, wo er
Pionierarbeiten mit Diagrammen und Tabellen zur
grafischen Illustration der Nachrichten leistete.
1963 wurde er Kunstredakteur des Sunday Times
Magazine, danach für kurze Zeit Design Direktor
und assoziierter Redakteur der Sunday Times und
ging schliesslich als Art Direktor und Chef-redakteur
zum Sunday Times Magazine zurück.
Er hat viele Auszeichnungen für Art Direktion
gewonnen, darunter die D&AD Silber- und
Goldpreise.

Helmut Rottke
Art Director G.G.K. Dusseldorf

Helmut Rottke studied art in Offenbach.
He started his career as a graphic designer with
Anton Stankowski but after two years he became an
art director in 1967. Since then he has worked in
Troost Advertising Agency, Dusseldorf, EBD&CDP
Dusseldorf, and in 1975 he joined GGK Dusseldorf.
He has won many national and international awards
for art direction and his work can also be seen in
European Illustration '76'77.

Helmut Rottke a étudié l'art à Offenbach.
Il a débuté dans sa carrière comme designer
graphique chez Anton Stankowski mais après deux
ans il est devenu Directeur artistique en 1967. Depuis
lors il a travaillé chez Troost Advertising Agency,
Dusseldorf, EBD&CDP Dusseldorf, et en 1975 il
est entré chez GGK Dusseldorf.
Il a reçu de nombreux prix nationaux et internation-
aux pour sa direction artistique et on peut aussi voir
son travail dans Illustration Européenne '76'77.

Helmut Rottke studierte Kunst in Offenbach.
Er begann seine Karriere als Grafiker bei Anton
Stankowski und wurde 1967 nach zwei Jahren Art
Direktor. Danach arbeitete er für die Troost Agentur
und EBD&CDP in Düsseldorf und ist seit 1975 bei
GGK Düsseldorf.
Er hat etliche nationale und internationale Preise für
Art Direktion gewonnen und seine Arbeit ist im
European Illustration Jahrbuch '76'77 erschienen.

Jacques Seguela
Creative Director Roux Seguela Cazac et Goudard

Jacques Seguela started his career as a journalist.
He worked as a reporter for 'Paris Match' and in
1960 was editor of a magazine dealing with the war
in Algeria. He later joined the France Soir leisure
magazine group and also wrote guide books for
Livre de Poche.
He commenced his career in advertising in 1964, as
an art director at the Delpire agency. He then became
creative director of Axe Publicité and in 1970 formed
his own agency with Bernard Roux. In 1973 Alain
Cayzac joined the company. He plans to open
branches in England and Spain in 1979 and in
New York in 1981.

Jacques Seguela a débuté dans sa carrière comme
journaliste. Il a travaillé comme reporter chez 'Paris
Match' et en 1960 a été rédacteur-en-chef d'un
magazine qui traitait de la guerre en Algérie. Il a
rejoint ensuite le groupe de magazines de loisirs de
France-Soir et il est l'auteur de guides pour Le
Livre de Poche.
Il a commencé sa carrière publicitaire en 1964,
comme Directeur artistique à l'agence Delpire. Puis
il est devenu Directeur de création pour Axe
Publicité et en 1970 a créé sa propre agence avec
Bernard Roux. En 1973 Alain Cayzec s'est joint à
eux. Il a l'intention d'ouvrir des succursales en
Angleterre et en Espagne en 1979 et a New-York
en 1981.

Jacques Seguela begann seine Karriere als Journalist.
Er arbeitete als Reporter für 'Paris Match' und wurde
1960 Redakteur einer Zeitschrift, die über den
Krieg in Algerien berichtete. Danach arbeitete er für
die France Soir Zeitschriftengruppe und schrieb
ausserdem Reiseführer für Livre de Poche.
Er begann seine Werbekarriere 1964 als Art Direktor
bei der Delpire Agentur, wurde dann Creative
Direktor der Axe Publicité und gründete 1970 seine
eigene Agentur zusammen mit Bernard Roux. Alain
Cayzac schloss sich 1973 an. Weitere Agenturen
sollen 1979 in England und Spanien und 1981 in
New York eröffnet werden.

Alan Waldie
Art Director
Collett Dickenson Pearce & Partners Limited

Alan Waldie studied at Farnham School of Art.
Over the last 20 years he has worked as an art
director in many famous advertising agencies,
including Anderson Advertising, Roger Pryer
Advertising, Brunnings, GS Royds, Allen, Brady &
Marsh and since 1968 Collett Dickenson Pearce &
Partners Limited.
He has been responsible for many well known
advertising campaigns including Benson & Hedges
and Heineken. He has won many awards for art
direction in particular D&AD Gold and Silver
awards.

Alan Waldie a été étudiant à la Farnham School of Art.
Depuis vingt ans il a travaillé comme Directeur
Artistique dans de nombreuses agences publicitaires
célèbres, y compris Anderson Advertising, Roger
Pryer Advertising, Brunnings, GS Royds, Allen,
Brady & Marsh et depuis 1968 chez Collett Dickenson
Pearce & Partners Limited.
Il a été le responsable de nombreuses campagnes
publicitaires très connues comme celles de Benson
& Hedges et Heineken. Il a reçu de nombreux prix
pour sa direction artistique et en particulier ceux
d'or et d'argent de la D&AD.

Alan Waldie wurde an der Farnham School of Art
ausgebildet.
In den letzten 20 Jahren hat er als Art Direktor in
vielen namhaften Werbeagenturen gearbeitet, u.a.
Anderson Advertising, Roger Pryer Advertising,
Brunnings, GS Royds, Allen, Brady & Marsh, und
seit 1968 Collett Dickenson Pearce & Partners
Limited.
Er ist verantwortlich für viele bekannte Werbekampagnen, wie z.B. Benson & Hedges und Heineken,
und hat etliche Auszeichnungen für Art Direktion
erhalten, einschliesslich der D&AD Gold- und
Silberpreise.

Illustrations: Adrian George

Editorial

This section includes illustrations for newspapers, magazines and all forms of periodical publications.

Magazines et Journaux

Cette section comprend des illustrations pour journaux, magazines et périodiques de toutes sortes.

Redaktionelle Graphik

Dieser Abschnitt umfasst Illustrationen für Zeitungen, Zeitschriften und andere regelmässig erscheinende Veröffentlichungen aller Art.

Artist/Artiste/Künstler
Sue Coe
Designer/Maquettiste/Gestalter
Derek Ungless
Assistant Art Director/Directeur
Artistique Adjoint/
Assistierender Art Direktor
Derek Ungless
Art Director/Directeur
Artistique
Robert Priest
Publisher/Editeur/Verlag
**Montreal Standard Publishing
Company**
Magazine illustration for a
feature about soccer violence,
"Soccer Wars" by Brian
Glanville, in 'Weekend
Magazine', April 1978. Acrylics.
Illustration de revue pour un
article sur la violence des
matchs de football "Soccer
Wars" (Les guerres de football)
par Brian Glanville, dans
'Weekend Magazine', avril 1978.
Acryliques.
Zeitschriftenillustration für
einen Artikel über
Gewalttätigkeit beim Fussball,
"Soccer Wars" (Fussball-Kriege)
von Brian Glanville, in 'Weekend
Magazine', April 1978. Acryl.

Artist/Artiste/Künstler
Milton Glaser
Designers/Maquettistes/
Gestalter
Louise Moreau
Robert Priest
Assistant Art Director/
Directeur Artistique Adjoint/
Assistierender Art Direktor
Derek Ungless
Art Director/Directeur
Artistique
Robert Priest
Publisher/Editeur/Verlag
**Montreal Standard Publishing
Company**
Magazine illustration for a
feature about athletic shoes,
"Something afoot" by Caitlin
Kelly, in 'Weekend Magazine',
April 1978. Ink and film.
Illustration de revue pour un
article sur les chaussures
d'athlètes, "Something afoot"
par Caitlin Kelly, dans
'Weekend Magazine', avril 1978.
Encre et film.
Zeitschriftenillustration für
einen Artikel über Sportschuhe,
"Something afoot" (Etwas ist im
Gange) von Caitlin Kelly, im
'Weekend Magazine', April 1978.
Tusche und Film.

Artist/Artiste/Künstler
Ralph Steadman
Designer/Maquettiste/Gestalter
Susan Howe
Art Editor/Rédacteur Artistique/
Kunstredakteur
Alison Danes
Art Director/Directeur
Artistique
Malti Kidia
Publisher/Editeur/Verlag
Penthouse Publications
Magazine illustration for
"The man who said too much"
by Donald Woods in 'Penthouse'
July 1978. Inks, in black and
white.
Illustration de revue pour
"The man who said too much",
(L'homme qui en a trop dit)
par Donald Woods dans
'Penthouse' juillet 1978. Encres,
en noir et blanc.
Zeitschriftenillustration für
"The man who said too much"
(Der Mann, der zuviel redete)
von Donald Woods, in
'Penthouse', Juli 1978. Tusche,
schwarzweiss.

Artist/Artiste/Künstler
Ralph Steadman
Designer/Maquettiste/Gestalter
Susan Howe
Art Editor/Rédacteur Artistique/
Kunstredakteur
Alison Daines
Art Director/Directeur
Artistique
Malti Kidia
Publisher/Editeur/Verlag
Penthouse Publications
Magazine illustration for
"Coming apart at the seams",
a discussion on European
devolution and the movement
away from a corporate identity to
smaller independent states, by
Hans Koning in 'Penthouse',
June 1978. Inks, in colour.
Illustration de revue pour
"Coming apart at the seams"
(Désintégration), discussion
sur la dévolution en Europe et
l'éloignement de l'idée d'une
identité unique vers des Etats
indépendants plus petits, par
Hans Koning, dans 'Penthouse',
juin 1978.
Encres, en couleurs.
Zeitschriftenillustration für
"Coming apart at the seams"
(Die Nähte reissen), eine
Diskussion über Devolution
in Europa und die Strömungen
von einer Gesamtidentität zu
kleineren, unabhängigen
Staaten, von Hans Koning, in
'Penthouse', Juni 1978. Tusche,
farbig.

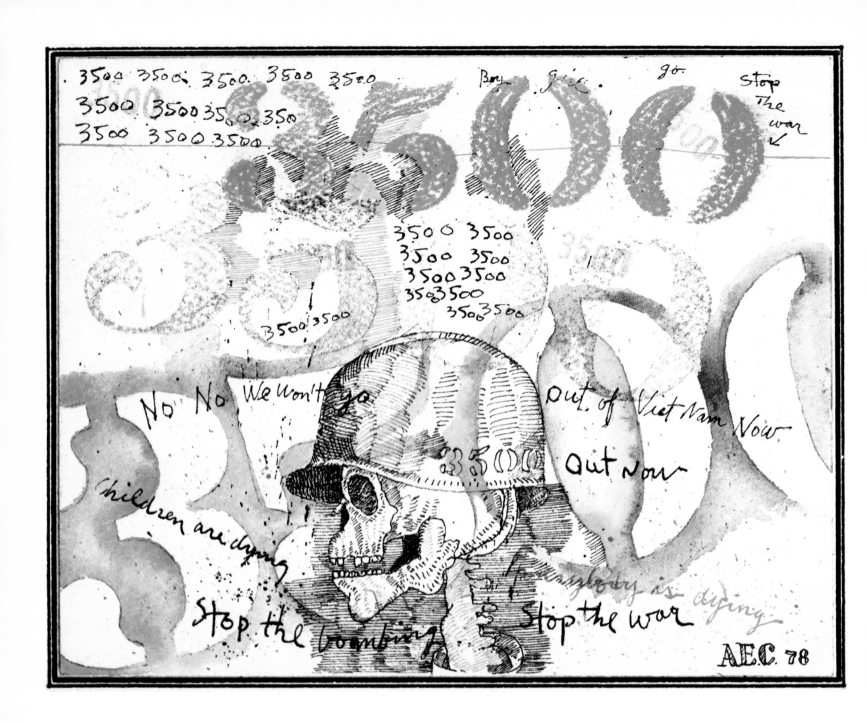

Artist/Artiste/Künstler
Alan E Cober
Designer/Maquettiste/Gestalter
Louise Moreau
Assistant Art Director/
Directeur Artistique Adjoint/
Assistierender Art Direktor
Derek Ungless
Art Director/Directeur Artistique
Robert Priest
Publisher/Editeur/Verlag
**Montreal Standard Publishing
Company**

Magazine illustrations for an
article, "Ten Years After
Aquarius" by Henry Fenwick, in
'Weekend Magazine', April 1978.
The brief was to illustrate the
lyrics of four songs from the
musical 'Hair' with emphasis on
racialism, pollution, narcotics,
and war. Inks.
Illustrations de revue pour un
article, "Ten Years After
Aquarius" (Dix ans après
Aquarius) par Henry Fenwick,
dans 'Weekend Magazine', avril
1978.
L'objet était d'illustrer les
paroles de quatre chansons du
musical 'Hair' qui soulignaient
le racisme, la pollution, les
narcotiques et la guerre. Encres.
Zeitschriftenillustrationen für
einen Artikel, "Ten Years After
Aquarius" (Zehn Jahre nach
Aquarius) von Henry Fenwick, in
'Weekend Magazine', April 1978.
Die Aufgabe war, vier Liedtexte
aus dem Musical 'Hair' zu
illustrieren, mit besonderer
Betonung auf Rassismus,
Verschmutzung, Rauschgift
und Krieg. Tusche.

Artist/Artiste/Künstler
Peter Le Vasseur
Illustration. Acrylic, in colour.
Illustration. Acrylique, en
couleurs.
Illustration. Acryl, farbig.

Artist/Artiste/Künstler
Peter Le Vasseur
Illustration. Gouache, in colour.
Illustration. Gouache, en
couleurs.
Illustration. Gouache, farbig.

Artist/Artiste/Künstler
Peter Brookes
Art Editor/Rédacteur Artistique
Kunstredakteur
David Driver
Publisher/Editeur/Verlag
BBC Publications Limited
Magazine cover illustration for the 'Radio Times' "Chinese Week", 4th–10th February 1978. Gouache.
Illustration de couverture de revue pour "Chinese Week" (Semaine chinoise) du 'Radio Times', 4–10 février 1978. Gouache.
Titelblattillustration für die 'Radio Times' "Chinese Week" (Chinesische Woche), 4.–10. Februar 1978. Gouache.

Artist/Artiste/Künstler
Guenther Thumer
Designer/Maquettiste/Gestalter
George Guther
Art Director/Directeur Artistique
Rainer Wörtmann
Publisher/Editeur/Verlag
Heinrich Bauer Verlag
Magazine illustration for a feature on sex morals in Germany, "Das Tabu" (Taboos) by Ernst Bornemann, in 'Playboy' German edition, March 1977. Oils.
Illustration de revue pour un article sur la morale sexuelle en Allemagne, "Das Tabu" (Le tabou) par Ernst Bornemann, dans 'Playboy', édition allemande, mars 1977. Huile.
Zeitschriftenillustration für einen Artikel über Sex-Moral in Deutschland, "Das Tabu" von Ernst Bornemann, in 'Playboy, deutsche Ausgabe, März 1977. Öl.

Artiste/Artiste/Künstler
Werner Hofmann
Designers/Maquettistes/
Gestalter
Hans Rudolf Bosshard
Werner Hofmann
Art Director/Directeur
Artistique
Dr Heinrich Rumpel
Publisher/Editeur/Verlag
Xylon, Switzerland
Magazine illustration for
'Xylon 39', a publication
specialising in wood cuts.
Woodcut, in black and white.
Illustration de revue pour
'Xylon 39', publication se
spécialisant dans les gravures
sur bois. Gravure sur bois, en
noir et blanc.
Zeitschriftenillustration für
'Xylon 39', eine Veröffentlichung,
die sich auf Holzschnitte
spezialisiert. Holzschnitt,
schwarzweiss.

Artist/Artiste/Künstler
Lionel Koechlin
Art Director/Directeur
Artistique
Monique Lanclud
Publisher/Editeur/Verlag
Societé Marie-Claire
Magazine illustration for an
article by Paule Giron about a
festival of mime which was
ruined by bad weather and
audience misunderstanding,
in 'Maison de Marie-Claire',
December 1977. Water-colour, in
black and white.
Illustration de revue pour un
article par Paule Giron sur
un festival de mime qui fut
gâché par le mauvais temps et
l'incompréhension du public
dans 'Maison de Marie-Claire'
décembre 1977. Aquarelle, en
noire et blanc.
Zeitschriftenillustration für
einen Artikel von Paule Giron
über ein Mimenfestspiel, das
durch schlechte Wetterverhält-
nisse und das Missverständnis
der Zuschauer ruiniert wurde, in
'Maison de Marie-Claire',
Dezember 1977. Wasserfarben,
schwarzweiss.

Artist/Artiste/Künstler
Guy Billout
Publisher/Editeur/Verlag
McCall's Publications
Magazine illustration for an
article, "The Meeting Game",
in 'Your Place', April 1978.
Water-colour.
Illustration de revue pour un
article "The Meeting Game",
(Le jeu des rencontres), dans
'Your Place', avril 1978. Aquarelle.
Zeitschriftenillustration für
einen Artikel, "The Meeting
Game" (Das Treff-Spiel), in
'Your Place', April 1978.
Wasserfarben.

Artist/Artiste/Künstler
Christian Piper
Designer/Maquettiste/
Gestalter
George Guther
Art Director/Directeur
Artistique
Rainer Wörtmann
Publisher/Editeur/Verlag
Heinrich Bauer Verlag
Magazine illustration for a
short story, "Bus Stop" by
Calder Willingham, in
'Playboy' German edition, April
1977. Mixed media.
Illustration de revue pour un
conte, "Bus Stop", (Arrêt
d'autobus) par Calder
Willingham, dans 'Playboy'
édition allemande, avril 1977.
Moyens divers.
Zeitschriftenillustration für eine
Kurzgeschichte, "Bus Stop" von
Calder Willingham, in 'Playboy',
deutsche Ausgabe, April 1977.
Mischtechnik.

Artist/Artiste/Künstler
Ralph Steadman
Art Editor/Rédacteur
Artistique/Kunstredakteur
David Driver
Publisher/Editeur/Verlag
BBC Publications
Magazine illustrations for a
feature, "The Hong Kong Beat"
by Anthony Lawrence, in
'Radio Times', 25th February
1978. Inks, in colour.
Illustrations de revue pour un
article, "The Hong Kong Beat"
(La ronde de Hong Kong) par
Anthony Lawrence, dans le
'Radio Times', 25 février 1978.
Encres, en couleurs.
Zeitschriftenillustrationen für
einen Artikel "The Hong Kong
Beat" (Der Pulsschlag
Hongkongs) von Anthony
Lawrence, in 'Radio Times',
25. Februar 1978. Tusche.
farbig.

Artist/Artiste/Künstler
Alex Murawski
Designers/Maquettistes/
Gestalter
Louise Moreau
Derek Ungless
Assistant Art Director/
Directeur Artistique Adjoint/
Assistierender Art Direktor
Derek Ungless
Art Director/Directeur
Artistique
Robert Priest
Publisher/Editeur/Verlag
Montreal Standard
Publishing Company
Magazine illustration for a
food feature, "Pacific Chicken"
by Margo Oliver, in
'Weekend Magazine', March
1978. Ink and gouache.
Illustration de revue pour un
article sur la cusine, "Pacific
Chicken" (Poulet du Pacifique)
par Margo Oliver, dans 'Weekend
Magazine', mars 1978. Encre et
gouche.
Zeitschriftenillustration für
einen Nahrungsmittel –Artikel,
"Pacific Chiken" (Pazifisches
Huhn) von Margo Oliver, im
'Weekend Magazine', März 1978.
Tusche und Gouache.

Artist/Artiste/Künstler
Peter Knock
Designers/Maquettistes/
Gestalter
Louise Moreau
Derek Ungless
Assistant Art Director/
Directeur Artistique Adjoint/
Assistierender Art Direktor
Derek Ungless
Art Director/Directeur
Artistique
Robert Priest
Publisher/Editeur/Verlag
**Montreal Standard Publishing
Company**
Magazine illustration for a
feature about the Queen's
presents, "Fit for a Queen" by
Alexander Frater, in 'Weekend
Magazine', April 1978, Water-
colour and pencil.
Illustration de revue pour un
article sur les cadeaux reçus
par la Reine, "Fit for a Queen"
(Dignes d'une Reine) par
Alexander Frater, dans
'Weekend Magazine', avril 1978.
Aquarelle et crayon.
Zeitschriftenillustration für
einen Artikel über die
Geschenke an die Königin,
"Fit for a Queen" (Geeignet für
eine Königin) von Alexander
Frater, im 'Weekend Magazine',
April 1978. Wasserfarben und
Bleistift.

Artist/Artiste/Künstler
Sue Coe
"How people commit suicide in
South Africa", a picture of
Steve Biko, influenced by the
illustrations of Ollie Harrington.
Gouache, in colour.
"How people commit suicide in
South Africa" (Comment on se
suicide en Afrique du Sud),
portrait de Steve Biko, influencé
par les illustrations de Ollie
Harrington. Gouache, en
couleurs.
"How people commit suicide in
South Africa" (Wie Menschen
in Südafrika Selbstmord
begehen), ein Bildnis Steve
Bikos, beeinflusst durch die
Illustrationen Ollie Harringtons.
Gouache, farbig.

Artist/Artiste/Künstler
Sue Coe
Designers/Maquettistes/
Gestalter
Louise Moreau
Robert Priest
Art Director/Directeur
Artistique
Robert Priest
Publisher/Editeur/Verlag
**Montreal Standard Publishing
Company**
Magazine illustration for a
feature, "Soldiers Of The Night"
by Jim Christy, in 'Weekend
Magazine', January 1978.
Acrylic, in colour.
Illustration de revue pour un
article "Soldiers of the Night"
(Les Soldats de la Nuit) par Jim
Christy, dans 'Weekend
Magazine', janvier 1978.
Acrylique, en couleurs.
Zeitschriftenillustration für
einen Artikel, "Soldiers Of The
Night" (Soldaten der Nacht) von
Jim Christy, in 'Weekend
Magazine', Januar 1978.
Acryl, farbig.

Artists/Artistes/Künstler
Peter Fluck
Roger Law
Photographer/Photographe/
Photograph
John Lawrence-Jones
Art Editor/Rédacteur Artistique/
Kunstredakteur
Peter Kleinman
Publisher/Editeur/Verlag
**National Lampoon
Incorporated**
Magazine illustrations for a
feature, "Euronazism" by
Tony Hendra, in 'National
Lampoon', February 1978.
Models.
Illustrations de revue pour
un article, "Euronazism"
par Tony Hendra, dans 'National
Lampoon', février 1978. Modèles.
Zeitschriftenillustrationen für
einen Artikel, "Euronazism"
(Euro-Nazismus) von Tony
Hendra, in 'National Lampoon',
Februar 1978. Modelle.

Artists/Artistes/Künstler
Peter Fluck
Roger Law
Photographer/Photographe/
Photograph
John Lawrence-Jones
Art Editor/Rédacteur Artistique/
Kunstredakteur
Peter Kleinman
Publisher/Editeur/Verlag
National Lampoon
Incorporated
Magazine illustration for a
feature, "Euronazism" by
Tony Hendra, in 'National
Lampoon', February 1978.
Models.
Illustration de revue pour
un article, "Euronazism"
par Tony Hendra, dans 'National
Lampoon', février 1978. Modèles.
Zeitschriftenillustration für
einen Artikel, "Euronazism"
(Euro-Nazismus) von Tony
Hendra, in 'National Lampoon',
Februar 1978. Modelle.

Artist/Artiste/Künstler
Julian Allen
Art Director/Directeur
Artistique
Regis Pajniez
Publisher/Editeur/Verlag
Playboy Enterprises
Magazine illustration for "The
Memoirs of Hitler's Barber" by
Woody Allen in 'Playboy', French
edition. Acrylic, in colour.
Illustration de revue pour "The
Memoirs of Hitler's Barber" (Les
Mémoires du Barbier d'Hitler)
par Woody Allen dans 'Playboy',
édition française. Acrylique, en
couleurs.
Zeitschriftenillustration für
"The Memoirs of Hitler's
Barber" (Die Memoiren des
Friseurs Hitlers) von Woody
Allen, in 'Playboy',
französische Ausgabe. Acryl,
farbig.

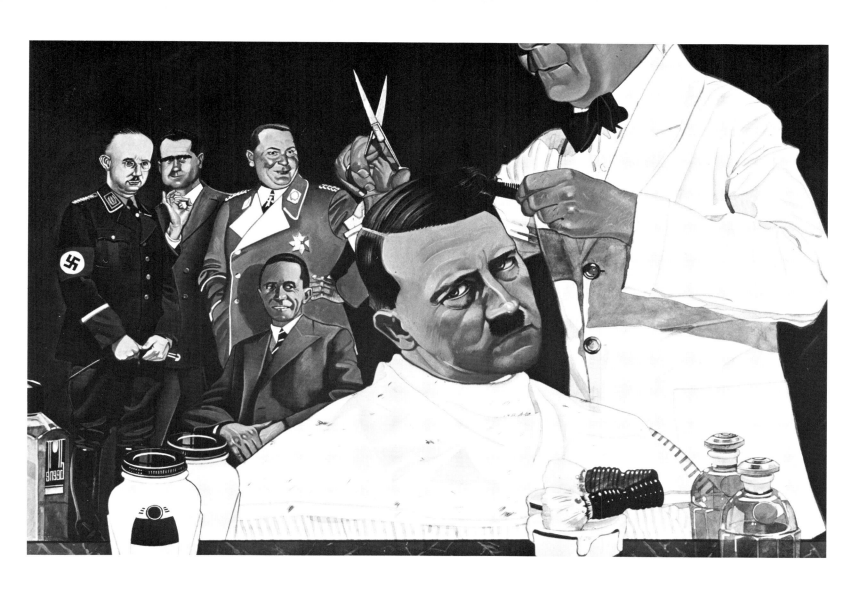

Artist/Artiste/Künstler
Julian Allen
Designer/Maquettiste/
Gestalter
Peter Blank
Art Director/Directeur
Artistique
Peter Blank
Publisher/Editeur/Verlag
Newsweek International
Magazine illustrations for "The
Ends of Power" by Bob
Haldeman in 'Newsweek',
27th February and 6th March
1978. Water-colour.
Illustrations de revue pour "The
Ends of Power" (Les fins du
Pouvoir) par Bob Haldeman
dans 'Newsweek', 27 février et
6 mars 1978. Aquarelle.
Zeitschriftenillustrationen für
"The Ends of Power" (Das Ende
der Macht) von Bob Haldeman,
in 'Newsweek', 27. Februar und
6. März 1978. Wasserfarben.

Artist/Artiste/Künstler
Robin Harris
Designer/Maquettiste/
Gestalter
Jeannette Collins
Art Director/Director
Artistique
Jeannette Collins
Publisher/Editeur/Verlag
Times Newspapers Limited
Newspaper illustration for a
novel extract about a man who
leaves a salaried profession in
broadcasting to become a
property developer, "The
Property Man" by Margaret
Drabble, in 'The Times
Saturday Review', 20th August
1977. Ink and wash, in black
and white.
Illustration de journal pour un
extrait de roman concernant
un homme qui quitte un poste
professionnel salarié pour se
faire promoteur immobilier,
"The Property Man" (Le
Promoteur) par Margaret
Drabble, dans 'The Times
Saturday Review', 20 août
1977. Encre et lavis en noir et
blanc.
Zeitungsillustration für einen
Romanauszug über einen
Mann, der eine gutbezahlte
Position im Rundfunk verlasst,
um Immobilienhändler zu
werden, "The Property Man"
(Der vermögende Mann) von
Margaret Drabble, in 'The
Times Saturday Review',
20 August 1977. Tusche laviert,
schwarzweiss.

Artist/Artiste/Künstler
Lawrence Mynott
Designers/Maquettistes/
Gestalter
John Hind
Lawrence Mynott
Art Director/Directeur
Artistique
John Hind
Publisher/Editeur/Verlag
The Royal College of Art
Magazine cover illustration
"The Modern Woman" for
'Ark' number 54, a journal
of the Royal College of Art.
Water-colour, gouache,
coloured pencil, in colour.
Illustration de couverture de
revue "The Modern Woman"
(La femme moderne) pour 'Ark'
numéro 54, une revue du Royal
College of Art. Aquarelle, gouache,
crayon de couleur, en couleurs.
Titelblattillustration "The
Modern Woman" (Die
Moderne Frau) für 'Ark' Nr. 54,
ein Journal des Royal College of
Art. Wasserfarben, Gouache,
Farbstifte, farbig.

Artist/Artiste/Künstler
Ralph Steadman
Designer/Maquettiste/
Gestalter
Geoff Axbey
Art Director/Directeur
Artistique
Geoff Axbey
Publisher/Editeur/Verlag
**The Sunday Telegraph
Limited**
A series of illustrations for a
feature, "A visit to Israel" by
Ralph Steadman, a portfolio of
personal impressions during
the visit of President Sadat of
Egypt, in the 'Telegraph Sunday
Magazine', 14th May 1978. Inks
and gouache.
Série d'illustrations pour un
article, "A visit to Israel" (Visite
en Israel) par Ralph Steadman,
carton d'impressions pendant
la visite du Président Sadat
d'Egypte, dans le 'Telegraph
Sunday Magazine', 14 mai 1978.
Encres et gouache.
Eine Serie von Illustrationen
für einen Artikel, "A visit to
Israel" (Eine Reise nach Israel)
von Ralph Steadman. Ein
Portfolio persönlicher Eindrücke
während des Besuches des
ägyptischen Präsidenten
Sadat, in 'Telegraph Sunday
Magazine', 14. Mai 1978.
Tusche und Gouache.

Ralph Steadman 77   Older Refugee Camp on the Gaza Strip

Artist/Artiste/Künstler
Ralph Steadman
Designer/Maquettiste/
Gestalter
Geoff Axbey
Art Director/Directeur
Artistique
Geoff Axbey
Publisher/Editeur/Verlag
**The Sunday Telegraph
Limited**
A series of illustrations for a
feature, "A visit to Israel" by
Ralph Steadman, a portfolio of
personal impressions during
the visit of President Sadat of
Egypt, in the 'Telegraph Sunday
Magazine', 14th May 1978. Inks
and gouache.
Série d'illustrations pour un
article, "A visit to Israel" (Visite
en Israel) par Ralph Steadman,
carton d'impressions pendant
la visite du Président Sadat
d'Egypte, dans le 'Telegraph
Sunday Magazine', 14 mai 1978.
Encres et gouache.
Eine Serie von Illustrationen
für einen Artikel, "A visit to
Israel" (Eine Reise nach Israel)
von Ralph Steadman. Ein
Portfolio persönlicher Eindrücke
während des Besuches des
ägyptischen Präsidenten
Sadat, in 'Telegraph Sunday
Magazine', 14. Mai 1978.
Tusche und Gouache.

New Refugee Camp - Gaza.   Ralph STEADman

Artist/Artiste/Künstler
Nick Taggart
Art Editors/Rédacteurs
Artistiques/Künstredakteure
Victoria Kogan
Steve Tyron
Art Director/Directeur
Artistique
Nick Taggart
Publisher/Editeur/Verlag
The American Art Review.
Magazine illustration for a
feature on the Los Angeles
work of Nick Taggart in 'The
American Art Review', June 1978.
Water-colour and gouache.
Illustration de revue pour un
article sur le travail de Nick
Taggart à Los Angeles dans
'The American Art Review',
juin 1978. Aquarelle et gouache.
Zeitschriftenillustration für
einen Artikel über Nick Taggarts
Los Angeles Arbeiten, in 'The
American Art Review', Juin 1978.
Wasserfarben und Gouache.

Artist/Artiste/Künstler
Erhard Göttlicher
Designer/Maquettiste/Gestalter
George Guther
Art Director/Directeur
Artistique
Rainer Wörtmann
Publisher/Editeur/Verlag
Heinrich Bauer Verlag
Magazine illustration for an
article about nude bathing in
Sylt, "Die Nackten und die
Blossen" (The naked and the
Bare) by Gunther Herburger, in
'Playboy', German edition.
Water-colour and pencil.
Illustration de revue pour un
article sur une baignade nue á
Sylt, "Die Nackten und die
Blossen" (Les Nus et les Décou-
verts) par Gunther Herburger,
dans 'Playboy', édition alle-
mande. Aquarelle et crayon.
Zeitschriftenillustration für
einen Artikel über Nacktbaden
auf Sylt, "Die Nackten und die
Blossen" von Gunther Herburger,
in 'Playboy', deutsche Ausgabe.
Wasserfarben und Bleistift.

Artist/Artiste/Künstler
Robin Harris
Design Editor/Rédacteur
Artistique/Kunstredakteur
Randall Goodall
Publisher/Editeur/Verlag
Point
Magazine back cover illustration
for 'Co Evolution Quarterly'
number 17 Spring 1978, featuring
a transcript of a conversation
betwwen Ken Kesey and
Governor Brown's office, "Cops
Without Guns". Acrylic, in
colour.
Illustration de dos de revue
pour 'Co Evolution Quarterly'
numero 17 printemps 1978,
donnant la transcription d'une
conversation entre Ken Kesey
et le bureau du Governor Brown,
"Cops Without Guns" (Flics
sans revolvers) Acrylique, en
couleurs.
Rückseitenillustration für 'Co
Evolution Quarterly', Nr. 17,
Frühjahr 1978, mit der Abschrift
einer Unterhaltung zwischen
Ken Kesey und Gouverneur
Browns Büro, "Cops Without
Guns" (Polizisten ohne Waffen).
Acryl, farbig.

Artist/Artiste/Künstler
Graham Dean
Designer/Maquettiste/Gestalter
George Guther
Art Director/Directeur
Artistique
Rainer Wörtmann
Publisher/Editeur/Verlag
Heinrich Bauer Verlag
Magazine illustration for an
article on terrorism in Northern
Ireland, "Irischer Sonntag"
(Irish Sunday) by Benedict Kiely,
in 'Playboy' German edition,
November 1977. Gouache, in
colour.
Illustration de revue pour un
article sur le terrorisme en
Irlande du Nord, "Irischer
Sonntag" (dimanche irlandais)
par Benedict Kiely, dans
'Playboy', édition allemande,
novembre 1977. Gouache, en
couleurs.
Zeitschriftenillustration für
einen Artikel über Terrorismus
in Nordirland, "Irischer Sonntag"
von Benedict Kiely, in 'Playboy',
deutsche Ausgabe, November
1977. Gouache, farbig.

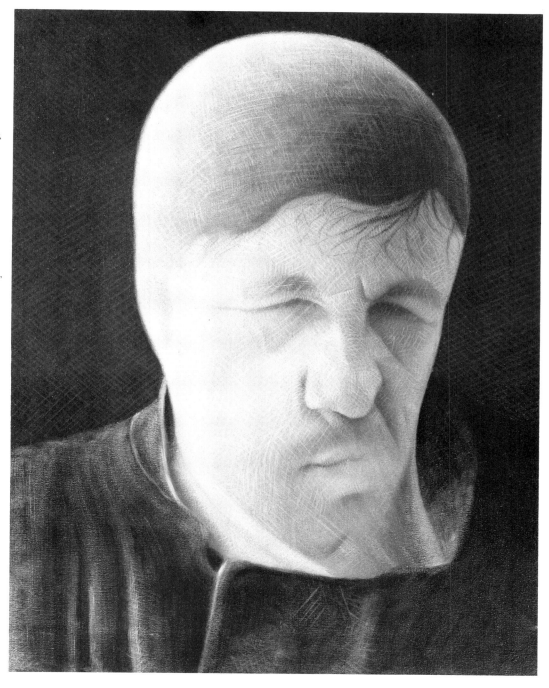

Artist/Artiste/Künstler
Philip Castle
Designer/Maquettiste/Gestalter
Philip Castle
Art Director/Directeur
Artistique
David Le Tissier
Publisher/Editeur/Verlag
Portfolio Graphics Limited
Original painting entitled "Truly
Trionic" used as a cover for
'Graphics World', March 1978,
featuring a profile of Philip Castle
by Douglas Mann. Gouache.
Tableau original intitulé "Truly
Trionic" qui a servi de couverture
pour 'Graphics World', mars
1978, contenant un profil de
Philip Castle par Douglas Mann.
Gouache.
Original Malerei mit dem Titel
"Truly Trionic", gezeigt auf dem
Titelblatt der 'Graphics World',
März 1978, mit einem Profil
Philip Castles von Douglas
Mann. Gouache.

Artists/Artistes/Künstlers
Mari Hofman
Kees Van Gelder
Art Director/Directeur
Artistique
Dick de Moei
Publisher/Editeur/Verlag
De Geillustreerde Pers BV
Amsterdam
Magazine illustration for a
fashion feature in 'Avenue', 1978.
Photo prints, aquarel pencils.
Illustration de revue pour un
article de mode dans 'Avenue'
1978. Clichés photographiques,
crayons aquarelle.
Zeitschriftenillustration für
einen Mode-Artikel in 'Avenue',
1978. Fotodruck, Aquarellstifte.

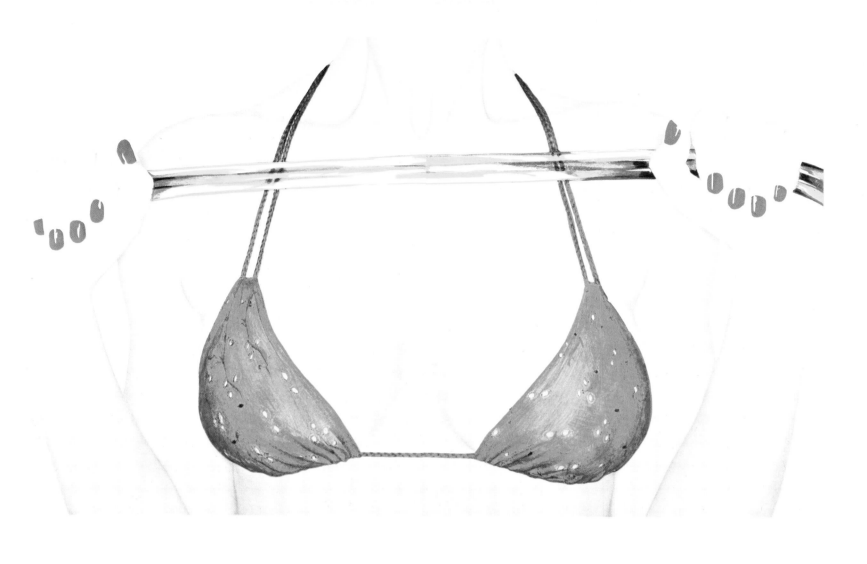

Artist/Artiste/Künstler
Jean Michel Renault
Art Director/Directeur
Artistique
Jean Michel Renault
Publisher/Editeur/Verlag
Editions D'Argaud
Magazine illustration in 'Pilote'
for an article on the American
Presidential election. Coloured
inks, in colour.
Illustration de revue dans
'Pilote' pour un article sur
l'élection présidentielle
américaine. Encres de couleurs
diverses, en couleurs.
Zeitschriftenillustration in
'Pilote' für einen Artikel über
die amerikanische Präsidenten-
wahl. Tusche, farbig.

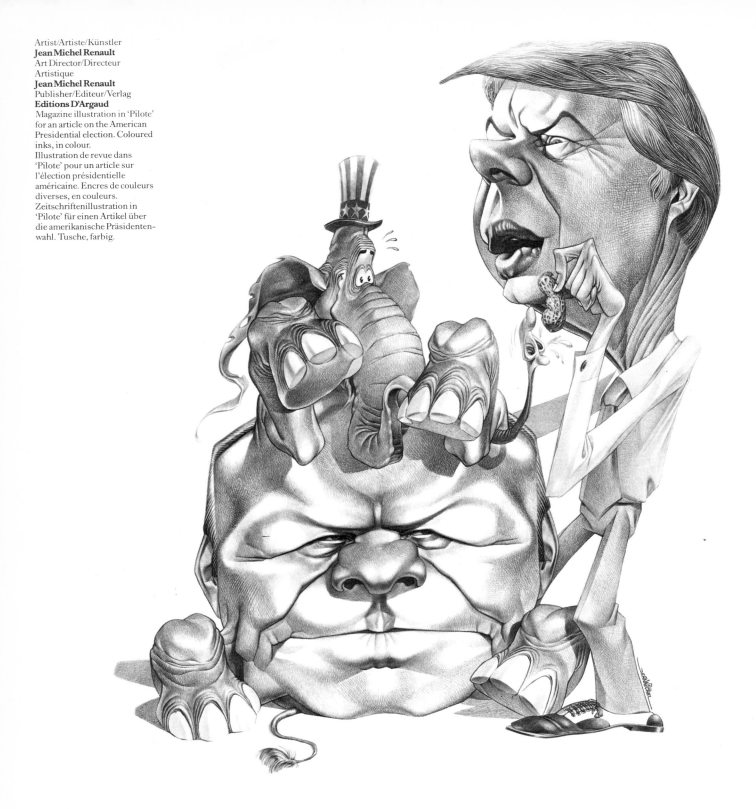

Artist/Artiste/Künstler
Etienne Delessert
Art Director/Directeur
Artistique
Martin Berthommiel
Publisher/Editeur/Verlag
Bayard Presse, Paris
Magazine illustration for an
article, "Vorster l'intransigeant"
(Vorster, the intransigent), in
'Record Magazine' Paris, 1977.
Inks and pencils, in colour.
Illustration de revue pour un
article, "Vorster l'intransigeant"
dans 'Record Magazine' Paris,
1977. Plumes et crayons, en
couleurs.
Zeitschriftenillustration für
einen Artikel, "Vorster l'intran-
sigeant" (Vorster, der Unnach-
giebige), in 'Record Magazine',
Paris, 1977. Tusche und
Farbstifte, farbig.

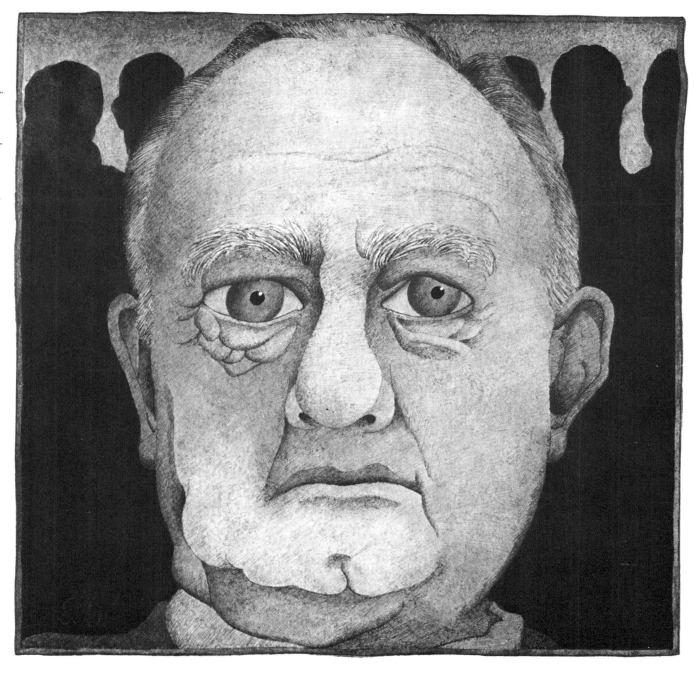

Artist/Artiste/Künstler
Alex Gnidziejko
Designers/Maquettistes/
Gestalter
Louise Moreau
Robert Priest
Assistant Art Director/
Directeur Artistique Adjoint/
Assistierender Art Direktor
Derek Ungless
Art Director/Directeur
Artistique
Robert Priest
Publisher/Editeur/Verlag
**Montreal Standard Publishing
Company**
Magazine cover illustration for
'Weekend Magazine' for an
issue featuring Billy Graham,
"King of the crusaders", by
Ken Lefolii. Acrylics.
Illustration de couverture de
revue pour 'Weekend Magazine'
pour un numéro sur Billy
Graham, "King of the
Crusaders" (Le Grand Apôtre
des campagnes morales) par
Ken Lefolii. Acryliques.
Titelblattillustration für
'Weekend Magazine' für einen
Artikel über Billy Graham, "King
of the Crusaders" (König der
Kreuzfahrer) von Ken Lefolii.
Acryl.

Artist/Artiste/Künstler
Marshall Arisman
Designers/Maquettistes/
Gestalter
Louise Moreau
Robert Priest
Assistant Art Director/
Directeur Artistique Adjoint/
Assistierender Art Direktor
Derek Ungless
Art Director/Directeur
Artistique
Robert Priest
Publisher/Editeur/Verlag
**Montreal Standard Publishing
Company**
Magazine illustration for a
feature, "Close encounters of the
monstrous kind" by Judith
Merrill, in 'Weekend Magazine',
April 1978. Ink.
Illustration de revue pour un
article, "Close encounters of the
monstrous kind" (Rencontres
du type monstrueux) par Judith
Merrill, dans 'Weekend
Magazine', avril 1978. Encre.
Zeitschriftenillustration für
einen Artikel "Close encounters
of the monstrous kind" (Nahe
Begegnungen der monströsen
Art) von Judith Merrill, im
'Weekend Magazine', April
1978. Tusche.

Artist/Artiste/Künstler
Arthur Robins
Designer/Maquettiste/Gestalter
John Tennant
Art Editor/Rédacteur
Artistique/Kunstredakteur
Clive Crook
Art Director/Directeur
Artistique
Michael Rand
Publisher/Editeur/Verlag
Times Newspapers Limited
Magazine illustration for an
article "Mother's Pride" by Mary
Kenny, in 'The Sunday Times
Magazine', 12th June 1977.
Water-colour, pen and ink, in
colour.
Illustration de revue pour un
article "Mother's Pride", par
Mary Kenny, dans 'The Sunday
Times Magazine', 12 juin 1977.
Aquarelle, plume, en couleurs.
Zeitschriftenillustration für
einen Artikel, "Mother's Pride"
(Mutters Stolz) von Mary Kenny,
in 'The Sunday Times
Magazine', 12. Juni 1977.
Wasserfarben, Feder und
Tusche, farbig.

Artist/Artiste/Künstler
Brian Froud
Designer/Maquettiste/Gestalter
David Larkin
Art Director/Directeur
Artistique
David Larkin
Publisher/Editeur/Verlag
Souvenir Press Limited
Harry N Abrams Incorporated
Book illustration for 'Faeries',
a history of Faerie in the form of
a full colour sketchbook with
notes by the contributing artists.
Published in September 1978.
Water-colour.
Illustration de livre pour
"Faeries" une histoire du pays
de la féerie sous forme d'une
carnet de croquis avec notes
des artistes participants. Publié
en septembre 1978. Aquarelle.
Buchillustration für 'Faeries',
die Geschichte des Faerie in
der Form eines farbigen Sketchbuchs mit Notizzen der
beteiligten Künstler. Erschienen
im September 1978.
Wasserfarben.

61

Artist/Artiste/Künstler
Erno Tromp
Art Director/Directeur
Artistique
Dick De Moei
Publisher/Editeur/Verlag
De Geillustreerde Pers BV
Amsterdam
Magazine illustration for a
feature on astrology in 'Avenue',
1978. Oils.
Illustration de revue pour un
article sur l'astrologie dans
'Avenue', 1978. Huile.
Zeitschriftenillustration für
einen Artikel über Astrologie,
in 'Avenue', 1978. Öl.

Artist/Artiste/Künstler
Jan Cremer
Designer/Maquettiste/Gestalter
Paul Röben
Art Director/Directeur
Artistique
Dick De Moei
Publisher/Editeur/Verlag
**De Geillustreerde Pers BV
Amsterdam**
Magazine illustration for a
feature on astrology in 'Avenue'.
Gouache.
Illustration de revue pour un
article sur l'astrologie dans
'Avenue'. Gouache.
Zeitschriftenillustration für
einen Artikel über Astrologie,
in 'Avenue'. Gouache.

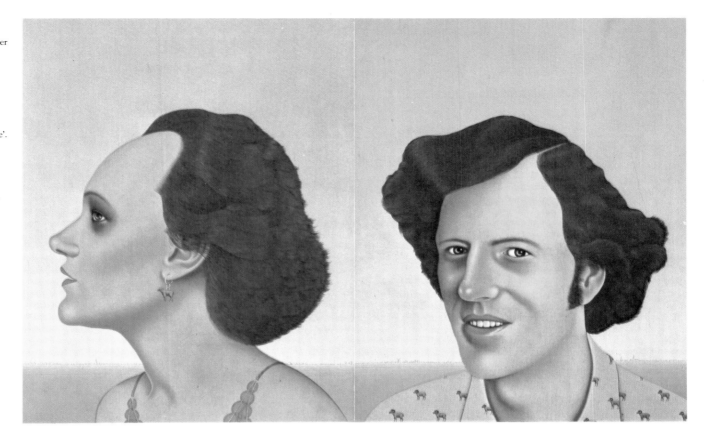

Artist/Artiste/Künstler
Nick Taggart
Art Editors/Rédacteurs
Artistiques/Kunstredakteure
Victoria Kogan
Steve Tyron
Art Director/Directeur
Artistique
Nick Taggart
Publisher/Editeur/Verlag
The American Art Review
Magazine illustration for a
feature on the Los Angeles
work of Nick Taggart in 'The
American Art Review', June
1978. "Mick Haggerty, Ros Cross
and Pinky outside their
Hollywood home". Water-
colour, gouache, some acrylic,
in colour.
Illustration de revue pour un
article sur le travail de Nick
Taggart à Los Angeles dans
'The American Art Review',
juin 1978. "Mick Haggerty,
Ros Cross and Pinky outside
their Hollywood home". (Mick
Haggerty, Ros Cross et Pinky
devant leur maison à
Hollywood). Aquarelle, gouache,
de l'acrylique, en couleurs.
Zeitschriftenillustration für
einen Artikel über Nick
Taggarts Los Angeles Arbeiten,
in 'The American Art Review',
Juni 1978. "Mick Haggerty, Ros
Cross and Pinky outside their
Hollywood home" (Mick
Haggerty, Ros Cross und Pinky
vor ihrem Haus in Hollywood).
Wasserfarben, Gouache, etwas
Acryl, farbig.

Artist/Artiste/Künstler
Nick Taggart
Art Editors/Rédacteurs
Artistiques/Kunstredakteure
Victoria Kogan
Steve Tyron
Art Director/Directeur
Artistique
Nick Taggart
Publisher/Editeur/Verlag
The American Art Review
Magazine illustration for a feature on the Los Angeles work of Nick Taggart in 'The American Art Review', June 1978. "Joe Pastori, Fruit Grower, Glassel Park, Los Angeles with Venice Background". Coloured pencils and water-colour, in colour.
Illustration de revue pour un article sur le travail de Nick Taggart à Los Angeles dans 'The American Art Review', juin 1978. "Joe Pastori, arboriculteur, Glassel Park, Los Angeles avec Venise en arrière-plan). Crayons de couleur et aquarelle, en couleurs.
Zeitschriftenillustration für einen Artikel über Nick Taggarts Los Angeles Arbeiten, in 'The American Art Review', Juni 1978. "Joe Pastori, Fruit Grower, Glassel Park, Los Angeles, with Venice Background". (Joe Pastori, Obstpflanzer, Glassel Park, Los Angeles, im Hintergrund Venedig). Farbstifte und Wasserfarben, farbig.

Artist/Artiste/Künstler
Peter Knock
Assistant Art Director/Directeur
Artistique Adjoint/
Assistierender Art Direktor
Derek Ungless
Art Director/Directeur
Artistique
Robert Priest
Publisher/Editeur/Verlag
**Montreal Standard Publishing
Company**
Magazine illustration for an
article about tax havens, "The
Ultimate Exemption" by
Nestor Repetski in 'Weekend
Magazine', April 1978. Pencil
and water-colour.
Illustration de revue pour un
article sur les refuges fiscaux
"The Ultimate Exemption" (La
dispense définitive) par Nestor
Repetski dans 'Weekend
Magazine', avril 1978. Crayon
et aquarelle.
Zeitschriftenillustration für
einen Artikel über steuerfreie
Gebiete, "The Ultimate
Exemption". (Die letzte
Befreiung) von Nestor Repetski,
in 'Weekend Magazine', April
1978. Bleistift und Wasserfarben.

Artist/Artiste/Künstler
Nick Taggart
"Susan Rogers, expatriate in
Santa Monica, California".
Coloured pencils.
"Susan Rogers, expatriate in
Santa Monica, California".
(Susan Rogers, expatriée à
Santa Monica, Californie).
Crayons de couleur.
"Susan Rogers, expatriate, in
Santa Monica, California"
(Susan Rogers, Auswanderer, in
Santa Monica, Kalifornien).
Farbstifte.

Artist/Artiste/Künstler
Brian Froud
Designer/Maquettiste/
Gestalter
David Larkin
Art Director/Directeur
Artistique
David Larkin
Publisher/Editeur/Verlag
Souvenir Press Limited
Harry N Abrams Incorporated
Book illustration for 'Faeries',
a history of Faerie in the form of
a full colour sketchbook with
notes by the contributing artists.
Published in September 1978.
Water-colour and coloured
pencil.
Illustration de livre pour
"Faeries", histoire du pays de la
féerie sous forme de carnet de
croquis avec notes des artistes
participants. Publié en
septembre 1978. Aquarelle et
crayons de couleurs.
Buchillustration für 'Faeries',
die Geschichte des Faerie in
der Form eines farbigen
Sketchbuchs mit Notizzen der
beteiligten Künstler. Erschienen
im September 1978.
Wasserfarben und Farbstifte.

Artist/Artiste/Künstler
Paul Sample
Designer/Maquettiste/
Gestalter
Paul Sample
Art Director/Directeur
Artistique
David Curless
Publisher/Editeur/Verlag
Haymarket Press Limited
Magazine cover illustration for
'Campaign', showing the
temptations on offer at
conferences and exhibitions.
Finally not published. Pen and
ink, in black and white.
Illustration de couverture de
revue pour 'Campaign'
montrant les tentations offertes
dans les conférences et
expositions. N'a pas été publiée.
Dessin à la plume, en noir et
blanc.
Titelblattillustration für
'Campaign' über die Anreize,
die bei Konferenzen und
Ausstellungen geboten werden.
Nicht veröffentlicht. Feder und
Tusche, schwarzweiss.

Artist/Artiste/Künstler
Roy Coombs
Designer/Maquettiste/Gestalter
Roy Coombs
Art Director/Directeur
Artistique
Stafford Cliff
Publisher/Editeur/Verlag
Habitat Designs Limited
Illustrated calendar for 1978.
Gouache.
Calendrier illustré pour 1978.
Gouache.
Illustrierter Kalender für 1978.
Gouache.

Artist/Artiste/Künstler
Larry Learmonth
Designer/Maquettiste/
Gestalter
Bob Marchant
Art Director/Directeur
Artistique
Bob Marchant
Publisher/Editeur/Verlag
**Conference & Exhibitions
Publications Limited**
Magazine cover illustration for
an inside feature article about
air taxis for 'Conference &
Exhibitions Magazine', May
1978. Oils, in colour.
Illustration de couverture de
revue pour un article dans la
revue sur les taxis de l'air pour
'Conferences & Exhibitions
Magazine', mai 1978. Huile, en
couleurs.
Titelblattillustration für einen
Artikel über Lufttaxen für
'Conferences & Exhibitions
Magazine', Mai 1978. Öl, farbig.

Artist/Artiste/Künstler
A Ramon Gonzalez Teja
Designer/Maquettiste/Gestalter
A Ramon Gonzalez Teja
Art Director/Directeur/
Artistique
A Ramon Gonzalez Teja
Publisher/Editeur/Verlag
Editora 2 SA
Magazine illustration for a
feature on plant communication
in 'Lui', April 1978. Water-
colour, ink and chalk, in colour.
Illustration de revue pour un
article sur la communication
entre plantes dans 'Lui', avril
1978. Aquarelle, encre et craie,
en couleurs.
Zeitschriftenillustration für
einen Artikel über
Kommunikation mit Pflanzen,
in 'Lui', April 1978.
Wasserfarben, Tusche und
Kreide, farbig.

Artist/Artiste/Künstler
André François
Art Director/Directeur
Artistique
Fouli Elia
Publisher/Editeur/Verlag
**Elle France Editions et
Publications SA**
Magazine cover illustration for
the Christmas issue of 'Elle',
1977. Mixed media, in colour.
Illustration de couverture de
revue pour le numéro de Noël
de 'Elle', 1977. Moyens divers,
en couleurs.
Titelblattillustration für die
'Elle' Weihnachtsausgabe 1977.
Mischtechnik, farbig.

Artist/Artiste/Künstler
Peter Fischer
Art Director/Directeur
Artistique
Hartmut Brückner
Publisher/Editeur/Verlag
Joh Jacobs & Co GmbH
Magazine illustration for an
article on Dutch tea recipes in
'Kontakt', October 1977.
Water-colour.
Illustration de revue pour un
article sur les recettes de thé
hollandaises dans 'Kontakt',
octobre 1977. Aquarelle.
Zeitschriftenillustration für
einen Artikel über holländische
Teerezepte, in 'Kontakt',
Oktober 1977. Wasserfarben.

Artist/Artiste/Künstler
Peter Fischer
Art Director/Directeur
Artistique
Hartmut Brückner
Publisher/Editeur/Verlag
Joh Jacobs & Co GmbH
Magazine illustration for a
feature on English tea in
'Kontakt', September 1977.
Water-colour.
Illustration de revue pour un
article sur le thé anglais dans
'Kontakt', septembre 1977.
Aquarelle.
Zeitschriftenillustration für
einen Artikel über englische
Teerezepte, in 'Kontakt',
September 1977. Wasserfarben.

Artist/Artiste/Künstler
Peter Fischer
Art Director/Directeur
Artistique
Wolfgang Behnken
Publisher/Editeur/Verlag
Gruner & Jahr AG
Magazine illustration for a
feature about lamb cookery in
'Stern', April 1978. Water-
colour, in black and white.
Illustration de revue pour un
article sur la préparation de
l'agneau pour la table dans
'Stern', avril 1978. Aquarelle,
en noir et blanc.
Zeitschriftenillustration für
einen Artikel mit Kochrezepten
für Hammelfleisch, in 'Stern',
April 1978. Wasserfarben,
schwarzweiss.

Artist/Artiste/Künstler
Peter Fischer
Art Director/Directeur
Artistique
Wolfgang Behnken
Publisher/Editeur/Verlag
Gruner & Jahr AG
Magazine illustration for a
cookery article about the
Empress Maria Theresa who
had a passion for puddings,
"Sünden von Format" (Heavy
sins) by Karlludwig Opitz, in
'Stern', April 1978. Water-
colour, in black and white.
Illustration de revue pour un
article de cuisine sur
l'Impératrice Maria Theresa
qui avait une passions pour les
puddings, "Sünden von Format"
(Péchés de taille) par Karlludwig
Opitz, dans 'Stern', avril 1978.
Aquarelle, en noir et blanc.
Zeitschriftenillustration für
einen Artikel mit Rezepten
über die Kaiserin Maria
Theresa, deren grosse
Leidenschaft Pudding war,
"Sünden von Format" von
Karlludwig Opitz, in 'Stern',
April 1978. Wasserfarben,
schwarzweiss.

Artist/Artiste/Künstler
Manfred Vogel
Designer/Maquettiste/Gestalter
Angie Bronder
Art Director/Directeur
Artistique
Rainer Wörtmann
Publisher/Editeur/Verlag
Heinrich Bauer Verlag
Magazine illustration for an
article, "Halbzeit" (Half time)
by Raimund Le Viseur, in
'Playboy' German edition,
May 1977. Oils.
Illustration de revue pour un
article, "Halbzeit" (Mi-temps)
par Raimund Le Viseur, dans
'Playboy', édition allemande,
mai 1977. Huile.
Zeitschriftenillustration für
einen Artikel, "Halbzeit" von
Raimund Le Viseur, in
'Playboy', deutsche Ausgabe,
Mai 1977. Öl.

Artist/Artiste/Künstler
Mariet Numan
Designer/Maquettiste/
Gestalter
Joke Westerman
Art Director/Directeur
Artistique
Dick De Moei
Publisher/Editeur/Verlag
**De Geillustreerde Pers BV
Amsterdam**
Magazine illustration "Messen"
(Knives) by Pia Van Boven in
'Avenue'. Coloured pencil.
Illustration de revue pour
"Messen" (Couteaux) par Pia
Van Boven dans 'Avenue'.
Crayon de couleurs.
Zeitschriftenillustration
"Messen" (Messer) von Pia
Van Boven in 'Avenue'.
Farbstifte.

Artiste/Artiste/Künstler
Hermann Degkwitz
Art Editor/Rédacteur
Artistique/Kunstredakteur
Hermann L Gremliza
Art Director/Directeur
Artistique
Georg v. Kieseritzki
Publisher/Editeur/Verlag
Neuer Konkret Verlag
Magazine illustration for an
article on the fall of Willi Brandt,
"Der Glanz ist weg" (Gone is the
glitter), in 'Konkret', September
1977. Water-colour, in colour.
Illustration de revue pour un
article sur la chute de Willi
Brandt, "Der Glanz ist weg"
(L'éclat a disparu) dans
'Konkret', septembre 1977.
Aquarelle, en couleurs.
Zeitschriftenillustration für
einen Artikel über den
Niedergang Willi Brandts, "Der
Glanz ist weg", in 'Konkret',
September 1977. Wasserfarben,
farbig.

Artist/Artiste/Künstler
Hermann Degkwitz
Art Editor/Rédacteur
Artistique/Kunstredakteur
Ulrich Blumenschein
Art Director/Directeur
Artistique
Dieter Eisenlau
Publisher/Editeur/Verlag
Burda Verlag
Magazine illustration "Der
eiserne Kanzler" (The Iron
Chancellor) in 'Bunte',
January 1977. Ink, in black and
white.
Illustration de revue "Der
eiserne Kanzler" (Le Chancelier
de Fer) dans 'Bunte', janvier
1977. Plume, en blanc et noir.
Zeitschriftenillustration "Der
eiserne Kanzler" in 'Bunte',
Januar 1977. Tusche,
schwarzweiss.

Artist/Artiste/Künstler
Lionel Koechlin
Art Director/Directeur
Artistique
Philippe Raquette
Publisher/Editeur/Verlag
Editions du Kiosque
Cartoon strip entitled
"L'Affaire Valstar" by Philippe
Paringaux in 'Rock & Folk',
September 1977. Water-colour.
Bande dessinée intitulée
"L'Affaire Valstar" par Philippe
Paringaux dans 'Rock & Folk',
septembre 1977. Aquarelle.
Karikaturstreifen mit dem
Titel "L'Affaire Valstar" von
Philippe Paringaux in 'Rock &
Folk', September 1977.
Wasserfarben.

PARKING DE L'ÉTOILE. LA LONGUE STUDEBAKER LUISANTE
DE DIDIER VALSTAR, LE MAGNAT DE LA BIÈRE, ATTEND DANS
L'OMBRE. SOUDAIN, LES PHARES CLIGNOTENT : UNE
BRÈVE, DEUX LONGUES. UN SIGNAL?

Qui pourrait soupçonner ces deux paisibles noctambules d'être les dangereux kidnappers que toutes les polices de France recherchent en vain?

Artist/Artiste/Künstler
Mick Brownfield
Designer/Maquettiste/Gestalter
Edith Boyer
Art Editor/Rédacteur
Artistique/Kunstredakteur
Clive Crook
Art Director/Directeur
Artistique
Michael Rand
Publisher/Editeur/Verlag
Times Newspapers Limited
Magazine illustration for the
'Lifespan' series, "Not In Front
Of The Children" by Gillian
Freeman in 'The Sunday Times
Magazine' May 15th 1977.
Gouache, ink and airbrush,
in colour.
Illustration de revue pour un
article intitulé "Not In Front Of
The Children" (Pas devant les
enfants) par Gillian Freeman,
partie de la série 'Lifespan' dans
'The Sunday Times Magazine'.
Gouache, encre et aerographe,
en coulers.
Zeitschriftenillustration für
einen Artikel, "Not In Front Of
The Children" (Nicht vor den
Kindern) von Gillian Freeman
innerhalb der 'Lifespan' Serie
in 'The Sunday Times Magazine'.
Gouache, Tusche und
Spritztechnik, farbig.

Artist/Artiste/Künstler
Guy Billout
Art Director/Directeur
Artistique
J C Suarès
Publisher/Editeur/Verlag
New York Magazine
Magazine cover illustration
for an inside feature article on
loneliness in 'New York', March
1978. Water-colour, in colour.
Illustration de couverture de
revue pour un article sur la
solitude paru dans 'New York',
mars 1978. Aquarelle, en
couleurs.
Titelblattillustration für einen
Artikel über Einsamkeit, in
'New York', März 1978.
Wasserfarben, farbig.

Artist/Artiste/Künstler
Sue Coe
Designers/Maquettistes/
Gestalter
Louise Moreau
Robert Priest
Art Director/Directeur
Artistique
Robert Priest
Publisher/Editeur/Verlag
**Montreal Standard Publishing
Company**
Magazine illustration for a
Canadian opinion poll about
seal hunting in 'Weekend
Magazine', March 1978.
Acrylic.
Illustration de revue pour un
sondage canadien concernant
la chasse au phoque dans
'Weekend Magazine', mars 1978.
Acrylique.
Zeitschriftenillustration für
eine Meinungsumfrage in
Kanada über die Robbenjagd,
in 'Weekend Magazine',
März 1978. Acryl.

Artist/Artiste/Künstler
Ralph Steadman
Designer/Maquettiste/Gestalter
Robert Priest
Art Director/Directeur
Artistique
Robert Priest
Publisher/Editeur/Verlag
**Montreal Standard Publishing
Company**
Magazine cover illustration for
'Weekend Magazine' for an issue
featuring "Seal Hunt" by Fred
Bruemmer, March 1978.
Ink.
Illustration de couverture de
revue pour 'Weekend Magazine'
pour un article sur "Seal Hunt"
(Chasse au phoque) par Fred
Bruemmer, mars 1978. Encre.
Titelblattillustration für
'Weekend Magazine' für einen
Artikel "Seal Hunt" (Robbenjagd)
von Fred Bruemmer, März 1978.
Tusche.

Artist/Artiste/Künstler
Josse Goffin
Designer/Maquettiste/Gestalter
Jean-Pierre Marsilly
Art Director/Directeur
Artistique
Josse Goffin
Publisher/Editeur/Verlag
Pub
Magazine cover illustration for
'Dossier Freelance', May 1977.
Water-colour, in colour.
Illustration de couverture de
revue pour 'Dossier Freelance',
mai 1977. Aquarelle, en couleurs.
Titelblattillustration für 'Dossier
Freelance', Mai 1977.
Wasserfarben, farbig.

Artist/Artiste/Künstler
Eric Tenney
Designer/Maquettiste/Gestalter
David Larkin
Art Director/Directeur
Artistique
George Davidson
Publisher/Editeur/Verlag
Avon Books
Illustration based on the book
'Watership Down' by Richard
Adams, for a calendar to be
published in 1979. Water-colour,
in colour.
Illustration inspirée du livre
'Watership Down' by Richard
Adams, pour un calendrier qui
sera publié en 1979. Aquarelle,
en couleurs.
Illustration basiert auf dem
Buch 'Watership Down' von
Richard Adams, für einen
Kalender für 1979.
Wasserfarben. farbig.

Artist/Artiste/Künstler
Pierre Le-Tan
Art Editor/Rédacteur
Artistique/Kunstredakteur
Jocelyn Gunnar
Publisher/Editeur/Verlag
CTW
Magazine illustration for "Cats
Cradle", an article teaching
children how to count in
'Sesame Street', 1978.
Water-colour.
Illustration de revue pour "Cat's
Cradle", article enseignant aux
enfants à compter dans 'Sesame
Street', 1978. Aquarelle.
Zeitschriftenillustration für
"Cat's Cradle" (Katzenwiege),
ein Artikel, der Kindern das
Zählen lehrt, in 'Sesame Street',
1978. Wasserfarben.

Artist/Artiste/Künstler
Martin Leman
Designer/Maquettiste/Gestalter
Edith Boyer
Art Editor/Rédacteur
Artistique/Kunstredakteur
Clive Crook
Art Director/Directeur
Artistique
Michael Rand
Publisher/Editeur/Verlag
Times Newspapers Limited
Magazine illustration for "Cats
and the Rat Pack" by Celia
Haddon, part of 'Lifespan' series
in 'The Sunday Times
Magazine', 9th October 1977.
Oils on wood.
Illustration de revue pour
"Cats and the Rat Pack" par
Celia Haddon, partie de la série
'Lifespan' dans 'The Sunday
Times Magazine, 9 octobre
1977. Huile sur bois.
Zeitschriftenillustration für
"Cats and the Rat Pack" (Katzen
und die Rattenmeure), von Celia
Haddon, innerhalb der 'Lifespan'
Serie in 'The Sunday Times
Magazine, 9 Oktober 1977.
Öl auf Holz.

Artist/Artiste/Künstler
Chlöe Cheese
Designer/Maquettiste/Gestalter
Edith Boyer
Art Editor/Rédacteur
Artistique/Kunstredakteur
Clive Crook
Art Director/Directeur
Artistique
Michael Rand
Publisher/Editeur/Verlag
Times Newspapers Limited
Magazine illustration for "A
Beginners Guide To The Grape",
part of 'Lifespan' series in 'The
Sunday Times Magazine'.
Coloured pencil, in colour.
Illustration de revue pour "A
Beginners Guide To The Grape"
(Guide pour débutants dans le
raisin), partie de la série
'Lifespan' dans 'The Sunday
Times Magazine'. Crayon de
couleur, en couleurs.
Zeitschriftenillustration für "A
Beginners Guide To The Grape"
(Ein Leitfaden über die
Weintraube für Anfänger),
innerhalb der 'Lifespan' Serie in
'The Sunday Times Magazine'.
Farbstifte, farbig.

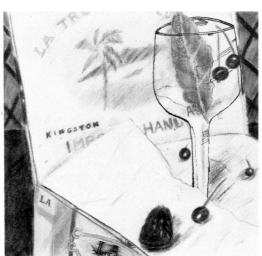

Artist/Artiste/Künstler
Chlöe Cheese
Designer/Maquettiste/Gestalter
John Tennant
Art Editor/Rédacteur
Artistique/Kunstredakteur
Clive Crook
Art Director/Directeur
Artistique
Michael Rand
Publisher/Editeur/Verlag
Times Newspapers Limited
Magazine illustration for an
article on picnics, "Al fresco à
la Française" by Caroline Conran,
in 'The Sunday Times Magazine'.
Crayon, in colour.
Illustration de revue pour un
article sur les pique-niques, "Al
Fresco à la Française", par
Caroline Conran, dans 'The
Sunday Times Magazine'.
Crayon de pastel, en couleurs.
Zeitschriftenillustration für
einen Artikel über Picknicks,
"Al Fresco à la Française" on
Caroline Conran, in 'The
Sunday Times Magazine'.
Crayon, farbig.

Artist/Artiste/Künstler
Adrian George
Designer/Maquettiste/Gestalter
Claudine Meissner
Art Editor/Rédacteur
Artistique/Kunstredakteur
David Driver
Publisher/Editeur/Verlag
BBC Publications Limited
Magazine illustrations for an
article, "Beside the Seaside"
by E S Turner, in 'Radio Times',
August 1977. Coloured crayons.
Illustrations de revue pour un
article, "Beside the Seaside"
(Au bord de la mer) par
E S Turner, dans 'Radio Times',
août 1977. Crayons de couleurs.
Zeitschriftenillustrationen für
einen Artikel, "Beside the
Seaside" (An der See) von
E S Turner, in 'Radio Times',
August 1977. Farbige Crayons.

POST CARD

THE ADDRESS ONLY TO BE WRITTEN ON THIS SIDE

POST CARD

THE ADDRESS ONLY TO BE WRITTEN ON THIS SIDE

Artist/Artiste/Künstler
Robert Mason
Art Director/Directeur
Artistique
Robert Priest
Publisher/Editeur/Verlag
Montreal Standard Publishing Company
Magazine illustration for a short story, "Spelling" by Alice Munro, in 'Weekend Magazine', June 1978. Mixed media, in colour.
Illustration de revue pour un conte "Spelling" (Orthographe) par Alice Munro, dans 'Weekend Magazine', juin 1978. Moyens divers, en couleurs.
Zeitschriftenillustration für eine Kurzgeschichte, "Spelling" (Buchstabieren) von Alice Munro, in 'Weekend Magazine', Juni 1978. Mischtechnik, farbig.

Artist/Artiste/Künstler
Russell Mills
Art Editor/Rédacteur
Artistique/Kunstredakteur
Clive Crook
Art Director/Directeur
Artistique
Michael Rand
Publisher/Editeur/Verlag
Times Newspapers Limited
Magazine illustration for an
article, "Marriage Bureaux–are
they bleeding the lonely
hearts?" by Carol Dix, in 'The
Sunday Times Magazine', 25th
September 1977. Mixed media,
in colour.
Illustration de revue pour un
article, "Marriage Bureaux–are
they bleeding the lonely hearts?"
(Les agences matrimoniales
sucent-elles à blanc les âmes
seules?) par Carol Dix, dans
'The Sunday Times Magazine',
25 septembre 1977. Moyens
divers, en couleurs.
Zeitschriftenillustration für
einen Artikel, "Marriage
Bureaux–are they bleeding the
lonely hearts?" (heirats-
institute–lassen sie einsame
Herzen bluten?) von Carol Dix
in 'The Sunday Times Magazine',
25. September 1977.
Mischtecknik, farbig.

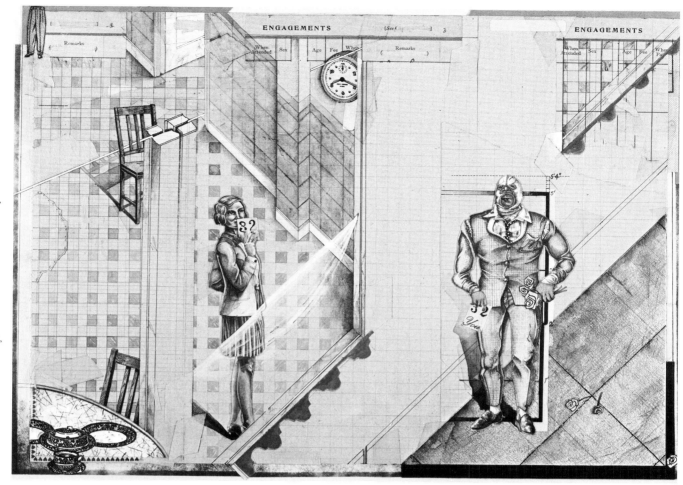

Artist/Artiste/Künstler
Peter Brookes
Designer/Maquettiste/Gestalter
John Tennant
Art Editor/Rédacteur
Artistique/Kunstredakteur
Clive Crook
Art Director/Directeur
Artistique
Michael Rand
Publisher/Editeur/Verlag
Times Newspapers Limited
Magazine illustration for "Home
Truths", part of the series
'Sacred Cows' in 'The Sunday
Times Magazine', 25th
September 1977. The brief was
to illustrate a piece highly
critical of the rôle of the building
societies. Gouache, in colour.
Illustration de revue pour
"Home Truths", partie de la
série 'Sacred Cows' dans 'The
Sunday Times Magazine' 25
septembre 1977. L'objet était
d'illustrer un article qui
critiquait très fort le rôle des
sociétés de prêts–logements.
Gouache, en couleurs.
Zeitschriftenillustration für
"Home Truths" (Binsen-
wahrheiten), innerhalb der
Serie 'Sacred Cows', in 'The
Sunday Times Magazine', 25.
September 1977. Die Aufgabe
war, einen äusserst kritischen
Artikel über die Rolle der
Bausparkassen zu illustrieren.
Gouache, farbig.

Artist/Artiste/Künstler
Peter Brookes
Designer/Maquettiste/Gestalter
John Tennant
Art Editor/Rédacteur
Artistique/Kunstredakteur
Clive Crook
Art Director/Directeur
Artistique
Michael Rand
Publisher/Editeur/Verlag
Times Newspapers Limited
Magazine illustration for "Beauty
and the Beast" by Mike Hill,
part of 'Lifespan' series in 'The
Sunday Times Magazine',
April 1977. Gouache, in colour.
Illustration de revue pour
"Beauty and the Beast" (La
Belle et la Bête) par Mike Hill,
partie de la série 'Lifespan' dans
'The Sunday Times Magazine',
avril 1977. Gouache, en couleurs.
Zeitschriftenillustration für
"Beauty and the Beast"
(Schönheit und das Tier) von
Mike Hill, innerhalb der
'Lifespan' Serie in 'The Sunday
Times Magazine', April 1977.
Gouache, farbig.

Artist/Artiste/Künstler
Peter Brookes
Designer/Maquettiste/Gestalter
Gilvrie Misstear
Art Director/Directeur
Artistique
Michael Rand
Publisher/Editeur/Verlag
Times Newspapers Limited
Magazine illustration for a quiz
on health and ageing, "The Good
Life Guide" by Tony Osman, in
'The Sunday Times Magazine',
December 1977. Pen and ink,
in black and white.
Illustration de revue pour une
enquête sur la santé et le
vieillissement, "The Good Life
Guide" (Un Guide pour vivre
bien) par Tony Osman, dans
'The Sunday Times Magazine',
décembre 1977. Dessin à la
plume, en noir et blanc.
Zeitschriftenillustration für
ein Fragespiel über Gesundheit
und Altern, "The Good Life
Guide" (Der Führer zum guten
Leben) von Tony Osman, in 'The
Sunday Times Magazine,
Dezember 1977. Feder und
Tusche, schwarzweiss.

Artist/Artiste/Künstler
Monica Polasz
Art Directors/Directeurs
Artistiques
Burckhardt Briese
Fee Zschocke
Publisher/Editeur/Verlag
Nelson Verlag, Hamburg
Magazine illustration for a
detective story, "Mings grösste
Beute" (Ming's biggest catch)
by Patricia Highsmith, in
'Katzen', May 1978. Pencil,
in black and white.
Illustration de revue pour roman
policier, "Mings grösste Beute"
(La plus grande prise de Ming)
par Patricia Highsmith, dans
'Katzen', mai 1978. Crayon, en
noir et blanc.
Zeitschriftenillustration für
eine Detektivgeschichte, "Mings
grösste Beute" von Patricia
Highsmith, in 'Katzen', Mai
1978. Bleistift, schwarzweiss.

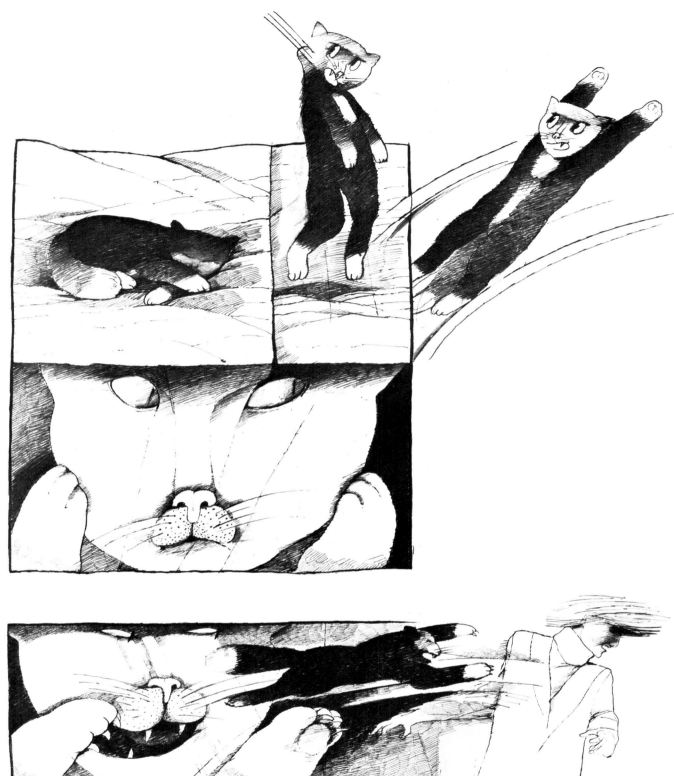

Artist/Artiste/Künstler
Pierre Le-Tan
Art Director/Directeur
Artistique
Lee Lorenz
Publisher/Editeur/Verlag
The New Yorker
Magazine cover illustration for
'The New Yorker', 27th February
1978. Water-colour, in colour.
Illustration de couverture de
revue pour 'The New Yorker',
février 1978. Aquarelle, en
couleurs.
Titelblattillustration für 'The
New Yorker', 27. Februar 1978.
Wasserfarben, farbig.

Artist/Artiste/Künstler
Pierre Le-Tan
Art Director/Directeur
Artistique
Lee Lorenz
Publisher/Editeur/Verlag
The New Yorker
Magazine cover illustration for
'The New Yorker', 14th November
1977. Water-colour, in colour.
Illustration de couverture de
revue pour 'The New Yorker',
14 novembre 1977. Aquarelle,
en couleurs.
Titelblattillustration für 'The
New Yorker', 14. November 1977.
Wasserfarben, farbig.

Artist/Artiste/Künstler
Russell Mills
Designers/Maquettistes/
Gestalter
Louise Moreau
Robert Priest
Derek Ungless
Assistant Art Director/Directeur
Artistique Adjoint/
Assistierender Art Direktor
Derek Ungless
Art Director/Directeur
Artistique
Robert Priest
Publisher/Editeur/Verlag
**Montreal Standard Publishing
Company**
Magazine illustration for a short
story, "The Muscle" by Barry
Callaghan, in 'Weekend
Magazine', April 1978. Ink and
collage, in colour.
Illustration de revue pour un
conte "The Muscle" (Le Muscle)
par Barry Callaghan, dans
'Weekend Magazine', avril 1978.
Dessin à la plume et collage,
en couleurs.
Zeitschriftenillustration für
eine Kurzgeschichte, "The
Muscle" (Der Muskel) von
Barry Callaghan, in 'Weekend
Magazine', April 1978. Tusche
und Collage, farbig.

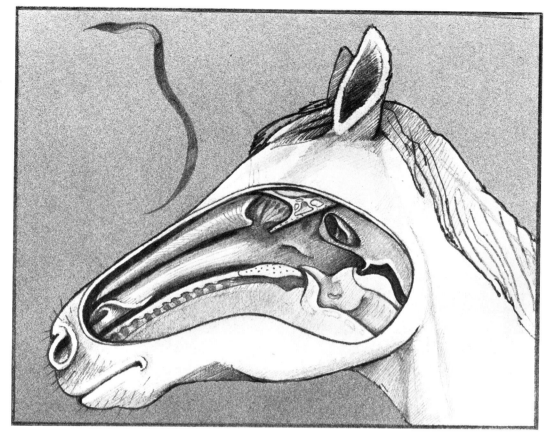

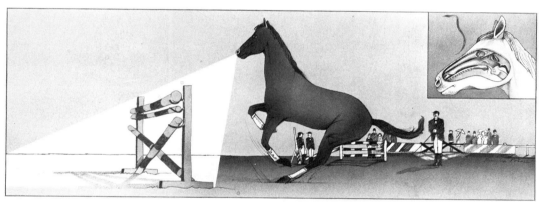

Artist/Artiste/Künstler
Monica Polasz
Designer/Maquettiste/Gestalter
Monica Polasz
Art Editor/Rédacteur
Artistique/Kunstredakteur
Wolfgang Schraps
Art Director/Directeur
Artistique
Wolfgang Behnken
Publisher/Editeur/Verlag
Gruner & Jahr AG
Magazine illustration for a series
"Ein Pferdeleben" (A Horse's
Life) by Wolfgang Schraps, in
'Stern'. Pencil, in black and white.
Illustration de revue pour une
série "Ein Pferdeleban"
(La Vie d'un cheval) par
Wolfgang Schraps, dans 'Stern'.
Crayon, en noir et blanc.
Zeitschriftenillustration für
eine Serie "Ein Pferdeleben"
von Wolfgang Schraps, in
'Stern'. Bleistift, schwarzweiss.

Artist/Artiste/Künstler
Gillian Platt
Art Editor/Rédacteur
Artistique/Kunstredakteur
Clive Crook
Art Director/Directeur
Artistique
Michael Rand
Publisher/Editeur/Verlag
Times Newspapers Limited
Magazine illustration for an
article entitled "Here Today,
Gone Tomorrow" by Graham
Rose, part of 'Lifespan' series
in 'The Sunday Times Magazine'.
Water-colour, in colour.
Illustration de revue pour un
article intitulé "Here Today,
Gone Tomorrow" par Graham
Rose, partie de la série 'Lifespan'
dans 'The Sunday Times
Magazine' Aquarelle, en
couleurs.
Zeitschriftenillustration für
einen Artikel, "Here Today,
Gone Tomorrow" (Heute hier,
morgen vergangen) von Graham
Rose, innerhalb der 'Lifespan'
Serie in 'The Sunday Times
Magazine'. Wasserfarben, farbig.

Artist/Artiste/Künstler
Peter Barrett
Art Director/Directeur
Artistique
Dom Rodie
Publicher/Editeur/Verlag
WH Allen Limited
Book cover illustration for 'The
Hare at Dark Hollow' by Joyce
Stranger. Water-colour, in
colour.
Illustration de couverture de
livre pour "The Hare at Dark
Hollow" (Le Lièvre à Dark
Hollow) par Joyce Stranger.
Aquarelle, en couleurs.
Buchumschlag für 'The Hare
at Dark Hollow' (Der Hase im
dunklen Tal) von Joyce Stranger.
Wasserfarben, farbig.

Artist/Artiste/Künstler
Joost Roelofsz
Designer/Maquettiste/Gestalter
Hans Van Blommenstein
Art Editor/Rédacteur
Artistique/Kunstredakteur
Maré Van Der Velde
Art Director/Directeur
Artistique
Dick De Moei
Publisher/Editeur/Verlag
De Geillustreerde Pers BV
Amsterdam
Magazine illustration for "Wat
Moet Dat Moet!" in 'Avenue',
August 1977. Water–colour, in
colour.
Illustration de revue pour "Wat
Moet Dat Moet!" dans 'Avenue',
août 1977. Aquarelle, en couleurs.
Zeitschriftenillustration für
"Wat Moet Dat Moet!" in
'Avenue', August 1977.
Wasserfarben, farbig.

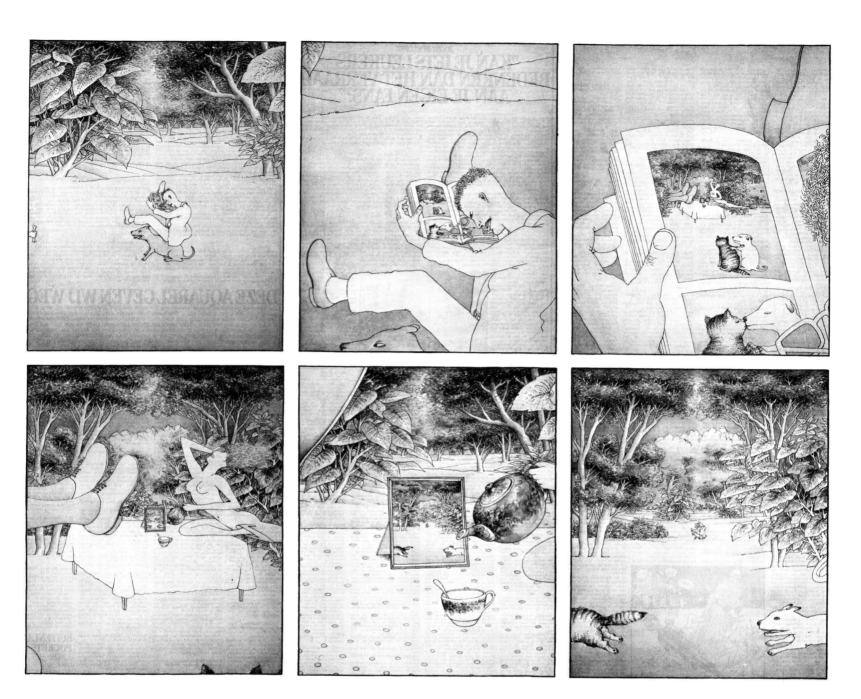

Artist/Artiste/Künstler
Barbara Lofthouse
"Metamorphosis".
Gouache, in colour.
"Metamorphosis„
(Métamorphose).
Gouache, en couleurs.
"Metamorphosis".
Gouache, farbig.

Artist/Artiste/Künstler
Rainer Cornelius Friz
Advertising Manager/Directeur
de la Publicité/Werbeleiter
Baukhard Rausch
Publisher/Editeur/Verlag
Heinrich Bauer Verlag
Certificate for winners of a road
safety competition run by
'Playboy', Gouache, in colour.
Certificat pour les gagnants d'un
concours de sécurité routière
organisé par 'Playboy'.
Gouache, en couleurs.
Urkunde für Gewinner eines
Fahrsicherheitslehrganges,
organisiert von 'Playboy'.
Gouache, farbig.

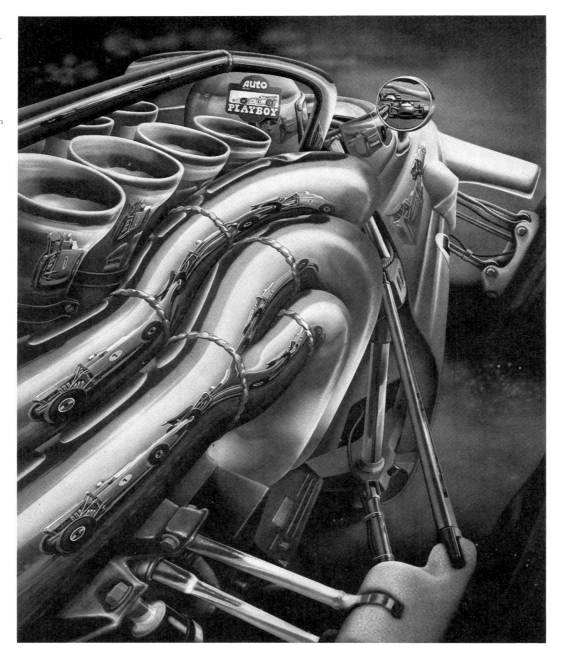

Books

This section includes work commissioned for book jackets, paperback covers, and all types of illustrated books, fiction and non-fiction.

Livres

Cette section comprend des travaux commandés pour des jacquettes de livres reliés, des couvertures de livres de poche, et tout sortes de livres illustrés.

Bücher

Dieser Abschnitt umfasst Arbeiten für Schutzumschläge, Paperback-Umschläge und Bücher aller Art, Romane und Sachbücher.

Artist/Artiste/Künstler
Roland Topor
Publisher/Editeur/Verlag
Editions Flammarion
Illustrations from a series of six
volumes, 'Oeuvres Roman-
esques' (Romantic Works), by
Marcel Aymé. Coloured pencil,
pen and ink, in colour.
Illustrations pour une série de
six volumes 'Oeuvres Roman-
esques,' par Marcel Aymé.
Crayon de couleur, plume et
encre, en couleurs.
Illustrationen innerhalb einer
Serie von sechs Bänden
'Oeuvres Romanesques'
(Romantische Werke) von
Marcel Aymé. Farbstifte, Feder
und Tusche, farbig.

Artist/Artiste/Künstler
Roland Topor
Publisher/Editeur/Verlag
Editions Flammarion
Illustrations from a series of six volumes, 'Oeuvres Romanesques' (Romantic Works), by Marcel Aymé. Coloured pencil, pen and ink.
Illustrations pour une série de six volumes 'Oeuvres Romanesques,' par Marcel Aymé. Crayon de couleur, plume et encre.
Illustrationen innerhalb einer Serie von sechs Bänden 'Oeuvres Romanesques' (Romantische Werke) von Marcel Aymé. Farbstifte, Feder und Tusche.

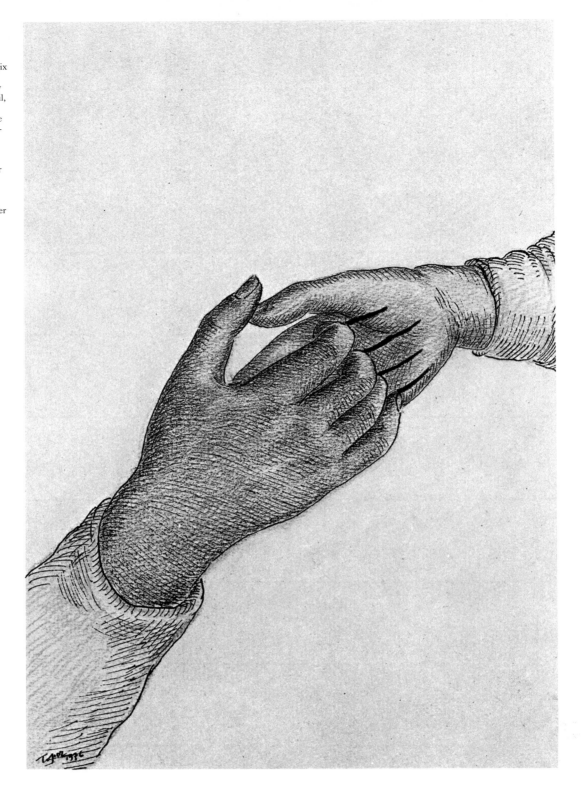

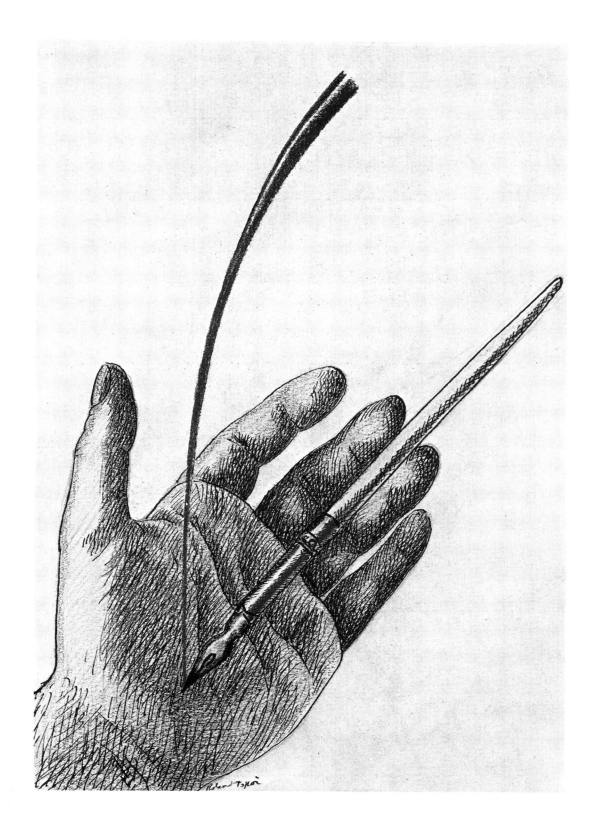

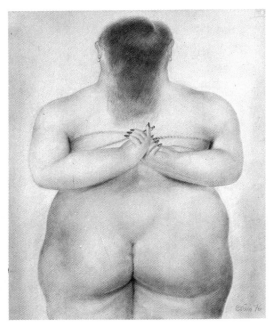

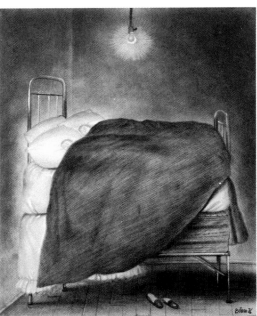

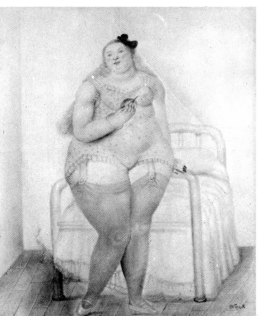

Artist/Artiste/Künstler
Fernando Botero
Art Director/Directeur
Artistique
Giorgio Soavi
Publisher/Editeur/Verlag
Ing C Olivetti & C SpA
Illustrations for the Olivetti
Diary, 1978. Water-colour and
pencil.
Illustrations pour l'agenda
Olivetti, 1978. Aquarelle et
crayon.
Illustrationen für den Olivetti
Terminkalender 1978. Wasser-
farben und Bleistift.

Artist/Artiste/Künstler
Marc Boxer
Designer/Maquettiste/
Gestalter
Mike Dempsey
Art Director/Directeur
Artistique
Mike Dempsey
Publisher/Editeur/Verlag
Fontana Paperbacks
Book cover illustration for 'At
Lady Molly's', one of a series of
twelve books 'A Dance to the
Music of Time' by Anthony
Powell, published in December
1977. Ink and coloured pencil,
in colour.
Illustration de couverture de
livre pour 'At Lady Molly's'
(Chez Lady Molly) l'un d'une
série de douze livres 'A Dance to
the Music of Time' (Dance sur
la musique des Temps) par
Anthony Powell, publiée en
décembre 1977. Encre et crayon
de couleur, en couleurs.
Paperback-Illustration für 'At
Lady Molly's' (Bei Lady Molly)
innerhalb einer Serie von zwölf
Büchern 'A Dance to the Music
of Time' (Ein Tanz zur Musik
der Zeit) von Anthony Powell,
erschienen Dezember 1977.
Tusche und Farbstifte, farbig.

Artist/Artiste/Künstler
Andrzej Krauze
Designer/Maquettiste/Gestalter
Andrzej Krauze
Publisher/Editeur/Verlag
Czytelnik
Illustration for 'New Happiness in Spray!' a collection of cartoons first published in 'Kultura' weekly magazine. Ink, in colour.
Illustration pour 'New Happiness in Spray' (Nouveau bonheur par aerosols) collection de dessins publiés en premier lieu dans la revue hebdomadaire 'Kultura.' Encre, en couleurs.
Illustration für 'New Happiness in Spray!' (Neues Glück im Spray!), eine Sammlung von Karikaturen, ursprünglich erschienen in der Wochenzeitschrift 'Kultura.' Tusche, farbig.

Artist/Artiste/Künstler
Joelle Boucher
Designers/Maquettistes/
Gestalter
Joelle Boucher
Jean Repailleau
Art Directors/Directeurs
Artistiques
Joelle Boucher
Jean Repailleau
Publisher/Editeur/Verlag
Editions GP
Book illustrations for
'Amandine Ou Les Deux
Jardins' (Amandine, or the two
 gardens) by Michel Tournier.
 Coloured inks.
Illustrations de livre pour
'Amandine ou les deux Jardins'
par Michel Tournier. Encres de
couleur.
Buchillustrationen für
'Amandine Ou Les Deux Jardins'
(Amandine oder die zwei
Gärten) von Michel Tournier.
Farbtusche, farbig.

Artist/Artiste/Künstler
Kevin W Maddison
Designer/Maquettiste/Gestalter
Kevin W Maddison
Art Director/Directeur
Artistique
Russell Ash
Publisher/Editeur/Verlag
Ash & Grant Limited
Illustration for a verse of
Edward Lear's poem 'The
Pobble Who Has No Toes,'
published October 1977.
Water-colour.
Illustration pour un vers du
poème d'Edward Lear 'The
Pobble Who Has No Toes,'
publié en octobre 1977.
Aquarelle.
Illustration für einen Vers des
Gedichts von Edward Lear
'The Pobble Who Has No Toes'
(Der Pobble, der keine Zehen
hat), erschienen Oktober 1977.
Wasserfarben.

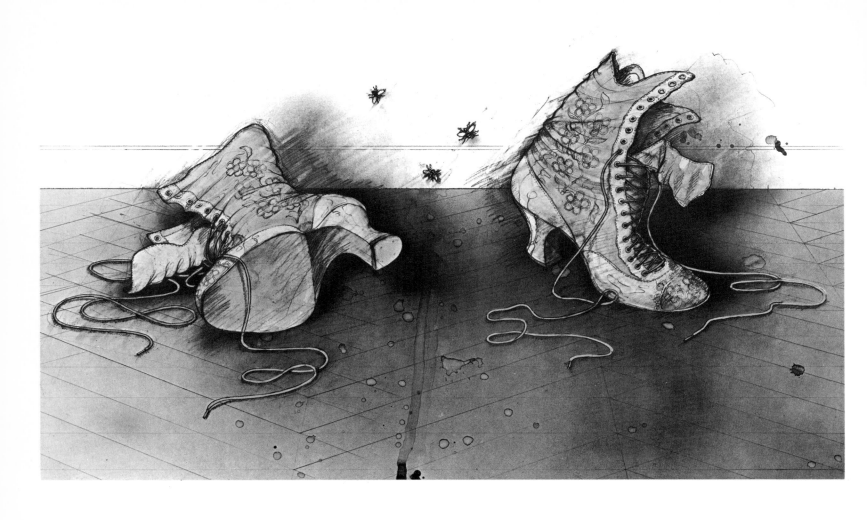

Artist/Artiste/Künstler
Erhard Göttlicher
Art Director/Directeur
Artistique
Juergen Seuss
Publisher/Editeur/Verlag
Büchergilde Gutenberg
Jacket and book illustrations for
'Nana' by Emile Zola. Pencil
and water-colour, in colour.
Jaquette de livre et illustrations
pour 'Nana' par Emile Zola.
Crayon et aquarelle, en couleurs.
Buchumschlag und Illustra-
tionen für 'Nana' von Emile Zola.
Bleistift und Wasserfarben,
farbig.

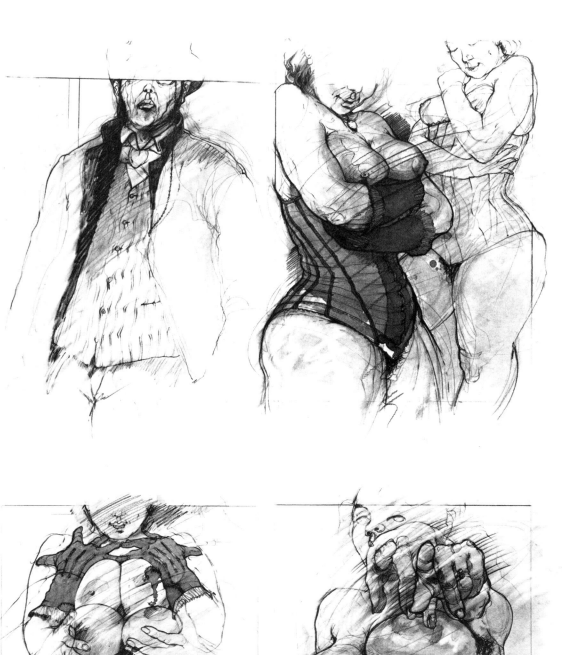

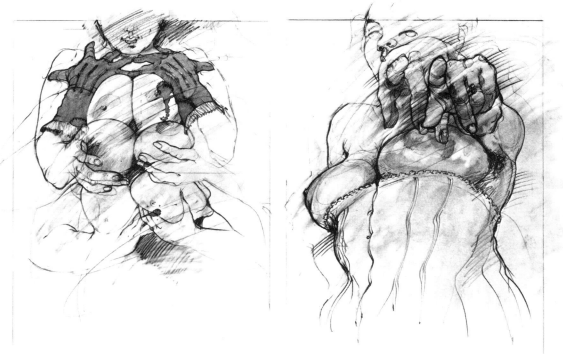

Artist/Artiste/Künstler
Robin Harris
Designer/Maquettiste/Gestalter
David Larkin
Art Director/Directeur
Artistique
David Larkin
Publisher/Editeur/Verlag
Picador Books
Book cover illustration for
'The Outsider' by Colin Wilson,
published in 1978. Gouache.
Illustration de couverture de
livre pour 'The Outsider' par
Colin Wilson, publié en 1978.
Gouache.
Buchumschlag für 'The
Outsider' (Der Aussenseiter)
von Colin Wilson, erschienen
1978. Gouache.

Artist/Artiste/Künstler
Adrian George
Designer/Maquettiste/Gestalter
Pearce Marchbank
Art Director/Directeur
Artistique
Pearce Marchbank
Publisher/Editeur/Verlag
Music Sales Limited
Book cover illustration for a
series of three classical guitar
music books. Crayon.
Illustration de couverture de
livre pour une série de trois
livres de musique pour guitare
classique. Crayon de pastel.
Buchumschlag für eine Serie
von drei Büchern über die
Musik der klassischen Gitarre.
Crayon.

Artist/Artiste/Künstler
Etienne Delessert
Designer/Maquettiste/Gestalter
Jean-Olivier Héron
Art Editor/Rédacteur
Artistique/Kunstredakteur
Jean-Robert Gaillot
Art Director/Directeur
Artistique
Pierre Marchand
Publisher/Editeur/Verlag
Editions Gallimard
Book cover illustration for
'Contes pour Enfants pas Sages'
(Stories for naughty children)
by Jacques Prévert, published
in the Folio Junior series in
1977. Mixed media, in colour.
Illustration de couverture de
livre pour 'Contes pour Enfants
pas sages' par Jacques Prévert,
publié dans la série Folio Junior
en 1977. Moyens divers, en
couleurs.
Buchumschlag für 'Contes pour
Enfants pas sages' (Geschichten
für unartige Kinder) von Jacques
Prévert, erschienen in der Folio
Junior Serie 1977. Mischtechnik,
farbig.

Artist/Artiste/Künstler
Ian Pollock
Art Editor/Rédacteur
Artistique/Kunstredakteur
Philip Dunn
Art Director/Directeur
Artistique
Philip Dunn
Publisher/Editeur/Verlag
Pierrot Publishing Limited
Book illustrations for 'The
Brothers of The Head' by Brian
Aldiss, published in December
1977. Water-colour and inks,
in colour.
Illustrations de livre pour 'The
Brothers of the Head' (Les frères
de la tête) par Brian Aldiss,
publié en décembre 1977.
Aquarelle et encres, en
couleurs.
Buchillustrationen für 'The
Brothers of The Head' (Die
Brüder des Kopfes) von Brian
Aldiss, erschienen Dezember
1977. Wasserfarben und Tusche,
farbig.

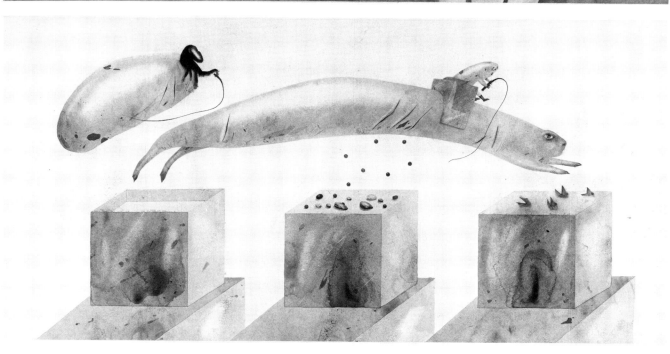

Artist/Artiste/Künstler
André Thijssen
Designer/Maquettiste/Gestalter
André Thijssen
Publisher/Editeur/Verlag
Agathon
Cover illustration for 'Herzog'
by Saul Bellow, published in
1977. Gouache, in colour.
Illustration de couverture pour
'Herzog' par Saul Bellow, publié
en 1977. Gouache, en couleurs.
Buchumschlag für 'Herzog' von
Saul Bellow, erschienen 1977.
Gouache, farbig.

Artist/Artiste/Künstler
André Thijssen
Designer/Maquettiste/Gestalter
André Thijssen
Publisher/Editeur/Verlag
Agathon
Book cover illustration for
'Seize the Day' by Saul Bellow,
published in 1978. Gouache,
in colour.
Illustration de couverture de
livre pour 'Seize the Day' (Saisir
le Jour) par Saul Bellow, publié
en 1978. Gouache, en couleurs.
Buchumschlag für 'Seize the
Day' (Machen Sie sich den Tag
zu Eigen) von Saul Bellow,
erschienen 1978. Gouache,
farbig.

Artist/Artiste/Künstler
Alan Lee
Designer/Maquettiste/Gestalter
David Larkin
Art Director/Directeur
Artistique
David Larkin
Publishers/Editeurs/Verlage
Souvenir Press Limited
Harry N Abrams Incorporated
Book illustrations entitled
"Finvarra" (top) and "Faerie
Combat" for 'Faeries', a history
of Faerie in the form of a full
colour sketch-book with notes
by the contributing artists.
Published in September 1978.
Water-colour, in colour.
Illustrations de livre intitulées
"Finvarra" (dessus) et "Faerie
Combat" pour 'Faeries' histoire
du pays de la féerie sous forme
de carnet de croquis en
couleurs, avec notes des artistes
participants. Publié en
septembre 1978. Aquarelle, en
couleurs.
Buchillustrationen mit den
Titeln "Finvarra" (oben) und
"Faerie Combat" für 'Faeries',
eine Geschichte des Zauber-
landes in der Form eines
farbigen Sketchbuchs mit
Notizzen der beteiligten
Künstler. Erschienen
September 1978. Wasserfarben,
farbig.

Artist/Artiste/Künstler
Tom Adams
Art Director/Directeur
Artistique
Anthony Colwell
Publisher/Editeur/Verlag
Jonathan Cape Limited
Book jacket illustration for
'Manwatching' by Desmond
Morris. The illustration is
intended to interpret the subject
of the title and incorporate the
image of a human eye reacting
with pleasure (shown by the
dilated pupil) to the image of
man. Acrylic, in colour.
Illustration de jaquette de livre
pour 'Manwatching' par
Desmond Morris. L'illustration
est censée interpréter le sujet du
titre et incorporer l'image de
l'oeil humain réagissant avec
plaisir (ce qui est démontré par
la pupille dilatée) à l'image de
l'homme. Acrylique, en
couleurs.
Buchumschlag für
'Manwatching' (Menschen-
beobachtung) von Desmond
Morris. Die Illustration ist eine
Interpretation des Titelthemas
und zeigt u.a. ein menschliches
Auge, das mit Freude auf das
Image Mensch reagiert
(illustriert durch die erweiterte
Pupille). Acryl, farbig.

Artist/Artiste/Künstler
Ralph Steadman
Designer/Maquettiste/Gestalter
Ralph Steadman
Publisher/Editeur/Verlag
**Andersen Press, London
Hutchinson, Australia**
Children's book illustrations
for 'Emergency Mouse' by
Bernard Stone, published in
1978. The artist's intention is
'to illustrate a book that will
sell millions, as part of a plan to
take over the world.' Inks.
Illustrations de livres d'enfants
pour 'Emergency Mouse' (La
souris d'urgence) par Bernard
Stone, publié en 1978. L'inten-
tion de l'artiste 'est d'illustrer un
livre qui se vendra par millions,
dans le but de gagner le monde.'
Encres.
Kinderbuchillustrationen für
'Emergency Mouse' (Die
Notfalls-Maus) von Bernard
Stone, erschienen 1978. Die
Absicht des Künstlers war, 'ein
Buch zu illustrieren, das
millionenfach verkauft wird, als
Teil eines Plans, die Welt zu
erobern.' Tusche.

134

Artist/Artiste/Künstler
Claude Lapointe
Designer/Maquettiste/Gestalter
Jean-Olivier Héron
Art Director/Directeur
Artistique
Pierre Marchand
Publisher/Editeur/Verlag
Editions Gallimard
Book illustration for 'La Guerre des Boutons' (The War of the buttons) by Louis Pergaud, published in December 1977. Pen and water-colour, in colour.
Illustration de livre pour 'La Guerre des Boutons' par Louis Pergaud, publié en décembre 1977. Encre et aquarelle.
Buchillustration für 'La Guerre des Boutons' (Der Kampf der Knöpfe) von Louis Pergaud, erschienen Dezember 1977. Feder und Wasserfarben, farbig.

Artist/Artiste/Künstler
Pier Canosa
Designer/Maquettiste/Gestalter
Roberto Rossini
Art Director/Directeur Artistique
Walter Basile
Publisher/Editeur/Verlag
Societa Editrice Ligure
Book illustration from 'Fiore 2103,' a book of fables by Lucetta Frisa, published in 1977. Water-colour, in colour.
Illustration de livre pour 'Fiore 2103,' livre de fables par Lucetta Frisa, publié en 1977. Aquarelle, en couleurs.
Buchillustration für 'Fiore 2103,' ein Buch von Fabeln von Lucetta Frisa, erschienen 1977. Wasserfarben, farbig.

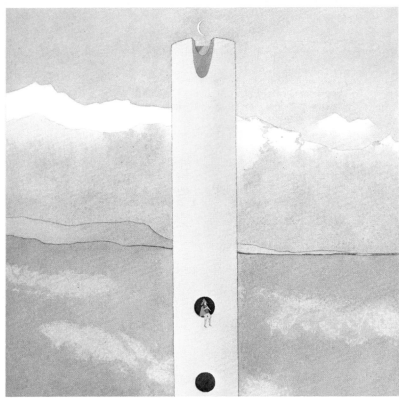

Artist/Artiste/Künstler
Georges Lemoine
Designer/Maquettiste/Gestalter
Georges Lemoine
Publisher/Editeur/Verlag
Chant du Monde
Book illustrations for 'Valse
pour Liseron' and 'Cerf Volant
de Lumière' by Uña Ramos, two
children's books with records.
Water-colour.
Illustrations de livres pour
'Valse pour Liseron' et 'Cerf
volant de lumière' par Uña
Ramos, deux livres d'enfant avec
disques. Aquarelle.
Buchillustrationen für 'Valse
pour Liseron' (Walzer für die
Winde) und 'Cerf Volant de
Lumière'(Der Papierdrache
des Lichts) von Uña Ramos,
zwei Kinderbücher mit
Schallplatten. Wasserfarben,
farbig.

Artist/Artiste/Künstler
Georges Lemoine
Designer/Maquettiste/Gestalter
Jean-Olivier Héron
Art Director/Directeur
Artistique
Pierre Marchand
Publisher/Editeur/Verlag
Editions Gallimard
Book illustration for 'L'Enfant
et la Rivière,' (The child and the
river) by Henri Bosco,
published December 1977.
Pen and water-colour.
Illustration de livre pour
'L'Enfant et la Rivière,' par
Henri Bosco, publié en
décembre 1977. Plume et
aquarelle.
Buchillustration für 'L'Enfant
et la Rivière' (Das Kind und
der Fluss) von Henri Bosco,
erschienen Dezember 1977.
Feder und Wasserfarben.

Artist/Artiste/Künstler
George Hardie
Designer/Maquettiste/Gestalter
George Hardie
Art Director/Directeur
Artistique
Storm Thorgerson
Publisher/Editeur/Verlag
Dragons World
Illustrations of an alphabet
used as chapter headings for
the book 'The Work of
Hipgnosis. "Walk Away René"'
by Storm Thorgerson. Ink and
gouache, pen and airbrush, in
colour.
Illustrations d'un alphabet
utilisées comme têtes de
chapitres pour un livre 'The
Work of Hipgnosis. "Walk away
René"' par Storm Thorgerson.
Encre et gouache, plume et
aérographe, en couleurs.
Illustrationen für ein Alphabet
von Kapitelüberschriften für
das Buch 'The Work of
Hipgnosis.' "Walk Away René"
(Hipgnosis Arbeiten, "Kehr den
Rücken, René") von Storm
Thorgerson. Tusche und
Gouache, farbig.

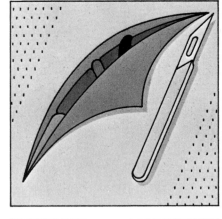
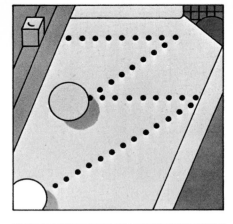

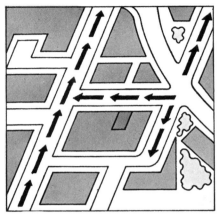
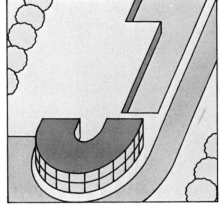
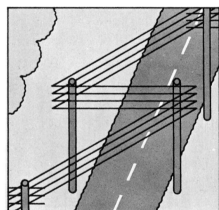
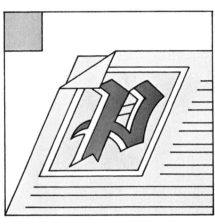
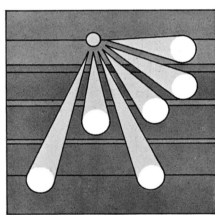
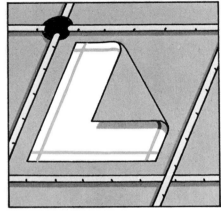

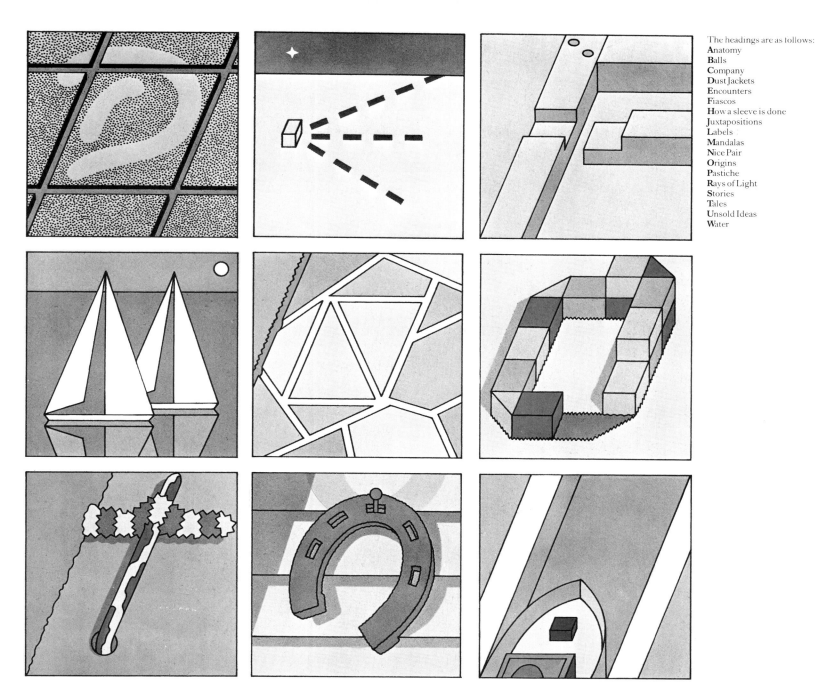

141

 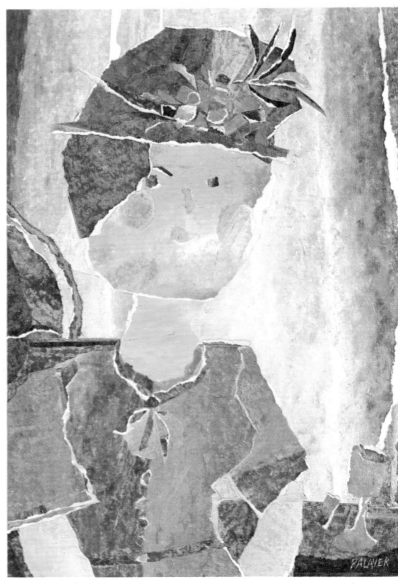

Artist/Artiste/Künstler
Jean Palayer
Art Director/Directeur
Artistique
Massin
Publisher/Editeur/Verlag
Club de l'Honnête Homme
Book illustrations for 'Fanny,
Marius, César' by Marcel Pagnol,
published in October 1977 as
part of a limited edition. Oil
pastel.
Illustrations de livre pour 'Fanny,
Marius, César' par Marcel
Pagnol, publié en octobre 1977
comme une partie d'édition
limitée. Pastel à l'huile.
Buchillustrationen für 'Fanny,
Marius, César' von Marcel
Pagnol, erschienen Oktober 1977
in numerierter Auflage. Öl,
Pastell.

Artist/Artiste/Künstler
Anne Howeson
Book illustration for 'A Paris
Diary' by Anne Howeson.
Crayon.
Illustration de livre pour
'A Paris Diary' (Journal de Paris)
par Anne Howeson. Crayon de
pastel.
Buchillustration für 'A Paris
Diary' (Ein Pariser Tagebuch)
von Anne Howeson. Crayon.

143

Artist/Artiste/Künstler
Ian Pollock
Designer/Maquettiste/Gestalter
Ian Pollock
Art Director/Directeur
Artistique
Philip Dunn
Publisher/Editeur/Verlag
Pierrot Publishing Limited
Illustration entitled "The
Recluse" for 'Beware of the Cat,'
a book of drawings of cats,
published in 1977. Radiograph,
pen and ink, in black and white.
Illustration intitulé "Le Reclus"
pour 'Beware of the Cat'
(Attention au chat), livre de
dessins de chats, publié en 1977.
Radiographie, plume et encre,
en noir et blanc.
Illustration mit dem Titel "Der
Einsiedler" für 'Beware of the
Cat' (Hüten Sie sich vor der
Katze), ein Buch mit Katzen-
zeichnungen, erschienen 1977.
Radiograph, Feder und Tusche,
schwarzweiss.

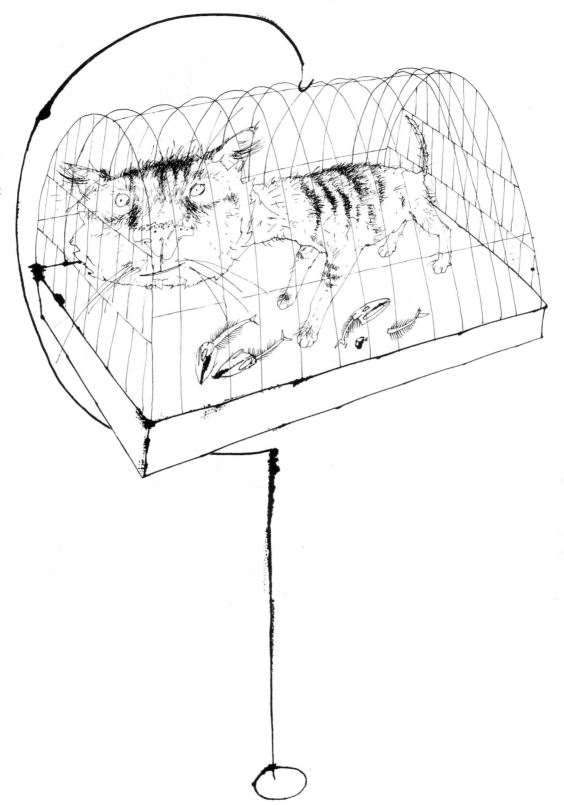

Artist/Artiste/Künstler
Heiner H Hoier
Designer/Maquettiste/Gestalter
Heiner H Hoier
Art Editor/Rédacteur Artistique/
Kunstredakteur
Roman Bala
Art Director/Directeur
Artistique
Heiner H Hoier
Publisher/Editeur/Verlag
Publico Dissense
Book illustration for 'November-
grün,' (November Green) by
Heiner Hoier, limited edition,
hand coloured, published in
March 1978. Magic marker, in
colour.
Illustration de livre pour
'Novembergrün' (Novembre
vert) par Heiner Hoier édition à
tirage limité, colorié à la main,
publié en mars 1978. Art marker,
en couleurs.
Buchillustration für 'November-
grün' von Heiner Hoier,
numerierte Auflage,
Handgezeichnet, erschienen
März 1978. Magic Marker, farbig.

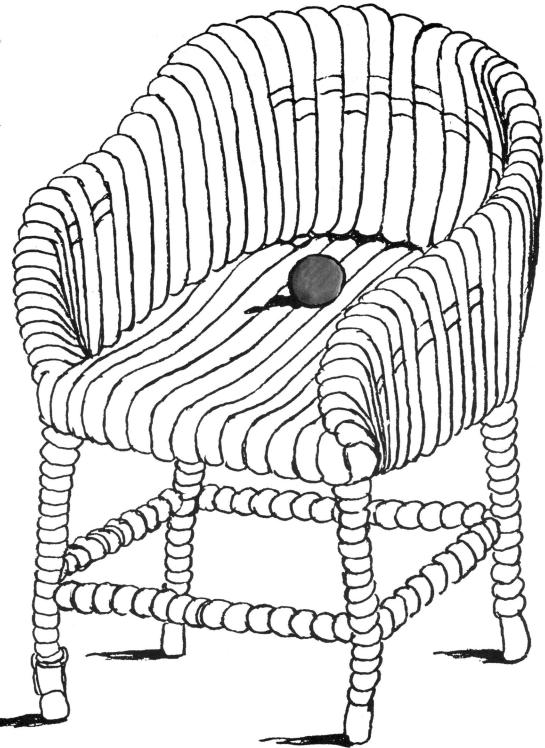

Artist/Artiste/Künstler
Peter Brookes
Designer/Maquettiste/ Gestalter
Peter Brookes
Art Director/Directeur
Artistique
David Pelham
Publisher/Editeur/Verlag
Penguin Books Limited
Book cover illustration for
'Hermit of Peking,' by Hugh
Trevor-Roper, published in
1978. The illustrator based his
drawing on classical Chinese
screens. Gouache, in colour.
Illustration de couverture de
livre pour 'Hermit of Peking'
(L'ermite de Pekin) par Hugh
Trevor-Roper, publié en 1978.
L'illustrateur a exécuté son
dessin d'après les écrans
classiques chinois. Gouache,
en couleurs.
Buchumschlag für 'Hermit of
Peking' (Der Einsiedler von
Peking) von Hugh Trevor-Roper,
erschienen 1978. Die Zeichnung
basiert auf klassischen
chinesischen Wandschirmen.
Gouache, farbig.

Artist/Artiste/Künstler
Tony Meeuwissen
Designer/Maquettiste/Gestalter
Tony Meeuwissen
Art Director/Directeur
Artistique
David Pelham
Publisher/Editeur/Verlag
Penguin Books Limited
Book cover illustration for 'The
Penguin Dictionary of British
Natural History,' by Richard and
Maisie Fitter. Water-colour.
Illustration de couverture de
livre pour 'The Penguin
Dictionary of British Natural
History' (Le Dictionnaire
Penguin d'histoire naturelle
anglaise), par Richard et Maisie
Fitter. Aquarelle.
Buchumschlag für 'The Penguin
Dictionary of British Natural
History' (Das Penguin Wörter-
buch der britischen Natur-
geschichte) von Richard und
Maisie Fitter. Wasserfarben.

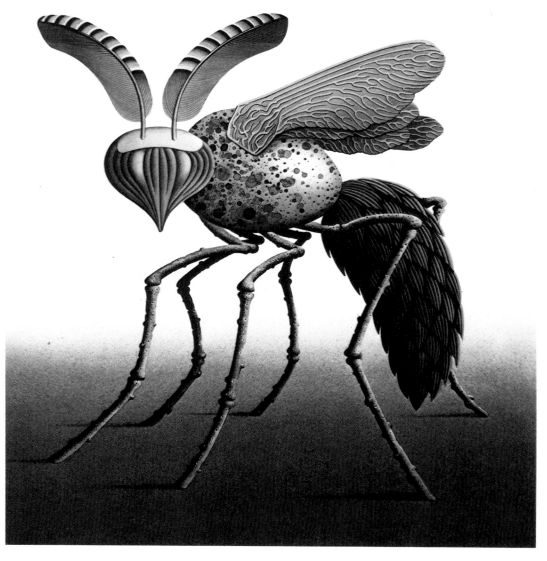

Artist/Artiste/Künstler
Donna Muir
Designer/Maquettiste/Gestalter
Donna Muir
Art Director/Directeur
Artistique
Pearce Marchbank
Publisher/Editeur/Verlag
Omnibus Press
Cover and illustrations for 'How to Dance', by Donna Muir, published in September 1977. The book features music and illustrated instructions for the following dances: Samba, Rumba, Bosanova, Waltz, Fox Trot, Tango, Cha Cha Cha, Jive, Mambo and Quick Step. Pen and ink, crayon and water-colour, in colour.
Couverture et Illustrations pour 'How to Dance' (Comment danser) par Donna Muir, publié en septembre 1977. Le livre présente de la musique et des instructions illustrées pour les danses suivantes: Samba, Rumba, Bosanova, Valse, Fox Trot, Tango, Cha Cha Cha, Jive, Mambo et Quick Step. Plume et encre, crayon de pastel et aquarelle, en couleurs.
Umschlag und Illustrationen für 'How to Dance' (So tanzt man) von Donna Muir, erschienen September 1977. Das Buch enthält Musik und illustrierte Anweisungen für die folgenden Tänze: Samba, Rumba, Bosanova, Walzer, Foxtrott, Tango, Cha Cha Cha, Jive, Mambo und Quickstep. Feder und Tusche, Crayon und Wasserfarben, farbig.

S.

1 MAN: L.F. FWD. (USE PIVOT ACTION TRNG. L.)
LADY: R.F. BACK (LONG STEP back.)

2. MAN: R.F. BACK (USE PIVOT ACTION TRNG L.)
LADY: L.F FWD. (STRONG STEP. FWD.)

1.
S.

S.

MAN: L.F FWD. (lead WITH TOE.)
LADY: R.F. BACK (long step back)

2. MAN: R.F FWD. (stay in line with PARTNER
LADY: L.F. back (long step back)

Q.
3.

MAN: L.F. SIDE. (Still turning, STEP toTOE.)
LADY: R.F SIDE. (KEEP CONTACT WITH PARTNER)

4.
S.

MAN: R.F. CLOSES TO L.F. (TURNING SQUARE TO PARTNER)
LADY: L.F. CLOSES TO R.F. (TURNING SQUARE TO PARTNER)

Magic step

3.
Q.

← 3. INST

MAN: R.F. FWD. (TAKE WEIGHT OVER TO) SIDE SIDE STEP.
LADY: R.F SIDE (KEEP CONTACT WITH PARTNER)

love you —

MAN: R.F. CLOSES TO L.F. (LOWERING TO HEELS.)
LADY: L.F. CLOSES TO R.F. (lowering to Heels)

latin' American shoes —

Good Luck and happy dancing

Latin American

Artist/Artiste/Künstler
Keleck
Designer/Maquettiste/Gestalter
Jean-Olivier Héron
Art Editor/Rédacteur Artistique/
Kunstredakteur
Hélène Charles
Art Director/Directeur
Artistique
Pierre Marchand
Publisher/Editeur/Verlag
Editions Gallimard
Book jacket illustration for
volume I in the series 'Récits et
Contes Populaires des Pyrénées'
(Popular Stories and Legends
from the Pyrenees) by Jean-
Pierre Pinies, published in
May 1978. Acrylic.
Illustration de jaquette de livre
pour le volume I dans la série
'Récits et Contes Populaires des
Pyrénées' par Jean-Pierre Pinies,
publié en mai 1978. Acrylique.
Buchumschlag für Band I der
Serie 'Récits et Contes
Populaires des Pyrénées'
(Erzählungen und Volksmärchen
der Pyrenäen) von Jean-Pierre
Pinies, erschienen Mai 1978.
Acryl.

Artist/Artiste/Künstler
Claude Lapointe
Designer/Maquettiste/Gestalter
Jean-Olivier Héron
Art Editor/Rédacteur Artistique/
Kunstredakteur
Hélène Charles
Art Director/Directeur
Artistique
Pierre Marchand
Publisher/Editeur/Verlag
Editions Gallimard
Book jacket illustration for
volume I in the series 'Récits et
Contes Populaires d'Auvergne'
(Popular Stories and Legends
from the Auvergne) by Marie-
Louise Teneze, published in
May 1978. Pen and water-colour.
Illustration de jaquette de livre
pour le volume I de la série
'Récits et Contes Populaires
d'Auvergne' par Marie-Louise
Teneze, publié en mai 1978.
Plume et aquarelle.
Buchumschlag für Band I der
Serie 'Récits et Contes
Populaires d'Auvergne'
(Erzählungen und Volksmärchen
der Auvergne) von Marie-Louise
Teneze, erschienen Mai 1978.
Feder und Wasserfarben.

Advertising
This section includes
work commissioned for
consumer, trade and
professional magazines
and newspapers.

Publicité
Cette section comprend
des travaux commandés
pour des magazines pro-
fessionels, de commerce,
de consommateurs et
pour des journaux.

Werbung
Dieser Abschnitt umfasst
Arbeiten für Werbung in
Verbraucher-, Handels-
und Fachzeitschriften
und in Zeitung.

Artist/Artiste/Künstler
Harry Hants
Designer/Maquettiste/Gestalter
Mark Williams
Art Director/Directeur
Artistique
Mark Williams
Copywriter/Rédacteur/Texter
Nick da Costa
Advertising Agency/Agence de
Publicité/Werbeagentur
**FGA/Kenyon & Eckhardt
Limited**
Client/Auftraggeber
RHM Foods Limited
Trade magazine advertisement,
"When it snows Saxa flows",
which appeared in 'The Grocer'.
Acrylic.
Publicité de revue
commerciale, "When it snows
Saxa flows" (Quand il neige
Saxa coule) parue dans 'The
Grocer'.
Acrylique.
Fachzeitschriftenwerbung,
"When it snows Saxa flows"
(Wenn es schneit, rieselt das
Saxa), erschienen in 'The
Grocer'.
Acryl.

Artist/Artiste/Künstler
Dorothee Walter
Art Director/Directeur
Artistique
Hannelore Gritz
Copywriter/Rédacteur/Texter
Ingrid Volkman
Advertising Agency/Agence de
Publicité/Werbeagentur
Doyle Dane Bernbach GmbH
Client/Auftraggeber
Beiersdorf AG, Hamburg
Magazine advertisement and
poster for Nivea creme, "Nivea,
wenn Ihnen die Haut Ihrer
kleinen Rothaut lieb ist" (Nivea,
if you care about the skin of
your little redskin). Also used
on a children's T-shirt with a
competition for children to win
an Indian headdress.
Water-colour.
Publicité de revue et affiche
pour la Crème Nivea, "Nivea
wenn Ihnen die Haut Ihrer
kleinen Rothaut lieb ist." (Nivea,
si vous aimez la peau de votre
petit Peau-rouge). Utilisée
également comme T-shirt
d'enfant avec concours pour
enfants permettant de gagner
une coiffure indienne.
Aquarelle.
Zeitschriftenwerbung und
Poster für Nivea Creme, "Nivea,
wenn Ihnen die Haut Ihrer
kleinen Rothaut lieb ist." Auch
auf T-shirts für Kinder
verwendet innerhalb eines
Wettbewerbs, in dem Kinder
indianischen Kopfschmuck
gewinnen konnten.
Wasserfarben.

Artist/Artiste/Künstler
Neil Patterson
Designer/Maquettiste/Gestalter
Neil Patterson
Art Director/Directeur
Artistique
John Hegarty
Copywriter/Rédacteur/Texter
Neil Patterson
Advertising Agency/Agence de
Publicité/Werbeagentur
TBWA Limited
Client/Auftraggeber
Newsweek International
Press advertisement, "How are
countries coping with
separatism?", to promote
'Newsweek's' coverage of
matters of general world interest.
Pentel and crayon, in full colour.
Publicité de presse, "How are
countries coping with
separatism?" (Comment les
pays font-ils face au
séparatisme?" pour souligner
l'importance des information de
'Newsweek' sur les questions
d'intérêt mondial.
Stylo bille Pentel et crayon de
pastel, en couleurs.
Pressewerbung für die
Nachrichtenübersicht zu
Themen von weltweitem
Interesse in 'Newsweek', "How
are countries coping with
separatism?" (Wie werden
Länder mit dem Problem der
Separatisten fertig?)
Pentel und Crayon, farbig.

Artist/Artiste/Künstler
Bob Wilson
Designer/Maquettiste/Gestalter
Alan Waldie
Art Director/Directeur
Artistique
Alan Waldie
Copywriter/Rédacteur/Texter
Mike Cozens
Advertising Agency/Agence de
Publicité/Werbeagentur
**Collett Dickenson Pearce &
Partners Limited**
Client/Auftraggeber
**Whitbread & Company
Limited.**
Press advertisement, "Heineken
refreshes the parts other beers
cannot reach." Charcoal pencil,
black and white.
Publicité de presse, "Heineken
refreshes the parts other beers
cannot reach." (Heineken
rafraîchit les endroits que les
autres bières ne peuvent
atteindre) Fusain, en noir et
blanc.
Pressewerbung, "Heineken
refreshes the parts other beers
cannot reach" (Heineken
erfrischt die Teile, die andere
Biere gar nicht erreichen).
Kohlstift, schwarzweiss.

Artist/Artiste/Künstler
Marina Clement
Art Director/Directeur
Artistique
Patrick Lepage
Advertising Agency/Agence de
Publicité/Werbeagentur
Publiscope
Client/Auftraggeber
Prêt à Porter
Magazine advertisement for
Prêt à Porter sports wear.
Oils.
Publicité de revue pour le Prêt à
Porter de vêtements de sport.
Huile.
Zeitschriftenwerbung für Prêt à
Porter Sportkleidung.
Öl.

Artist/Artiste/Künstler
Jooce Garrett
Designer/Maquettiste/Gestalter
Wim Bartels
Art Director/Directeur
Artistique
Wim Bartels
Advertising Agency/Agency de
Publicité/Werbeagentur
Franzen Hey & Veltman/BBDO
Client/Auftraggeber
Heineken Nederland NZ
International magazine
advertisement, "Unfailing good
taste in a 17th century
Amsterdam canal house.
Original Delft tiles on fireplace,
each painted with children's
games, solid walnut clothes
cupboard, 17th century chair
with hidden drawer under the
seat . . . and the authentic taste
of today's Heineken."
Acrylic.
Publicité de revue
internationale, (L'infailible bon
goût d'une maison du 17e siècle
au bord d'un canal d'Amsterdam.
Tuiles de Delft originales autour
de la cheminée, chacune peinte
d'un jeu d'enfant, armoire en
bois de noyer, chaise du 17e
siècle avec un tiroir caché sous
le siège . . . et le goût
authentique de la Heineken
d'aujourd'hui.)
Acrylique.
Internationale Zeitschriftenwerbung, (Unfehlbar guter
Geschmack in einem
Amsterdamer Grachtenhaus des
17. Jahrhunderts. Original Delft
Kacheln am Kamin, bemalt mit
Kinderspielen, massive
Nussbaum-Kleider schränke,
Stuhl mit versteckter Schublade
unter dem Sitz aus dem 17.
Jahrhundert . . . und der echte
Geschmack des heutigen
Heineken).
Acryl, farbig.

Artist/Artiste/Künstler
Arnold Schwartzman
Art Director/Directeur
Artistique
Bruce Gill
Advertising Agency/Agence de
Publicité/Werbeagentur
**Fletcher Shelton Delaney
& Reynolds Limited**
Press advertisement,
commissioned but not
published.
Pencil, in black and white.
Publicité de presse,
commandée mais non publiée.
Crayon, en noir et blanc.
Pressewerbung, in Auftrag
gegeben, aber nicht
veröffentlicht.
Bleistift, schwarzweiss.

Artist/Artiste/Künstler
Titus
Art Director/Directeur
Artistique
Marc Gaillard
Copywriter/Rédacteur/Texter
Thierry Colignon
Advertising Agency/Agence de
Publicité/Werbeagentur
Havas Conseil
Client/Auftraggeber
Air France
Magazine advertisement,
"Embrassez toute l'Amérique
du Sud avec Air France"
(Encircle South America with
Air France). Part of a series of
advertisements to promote the
Air France network.
Oils and acrylic.
Publicité de presse, "Embrassez
toute l'Amérique du Sud avec
Air France." Partie d'une
campagne de publicité au profit
du réseau Air France.
Huile et acrylique.
Zeitschriftenwerbung,
"Embrassez toute l'Amérique
du Sud avec Air France"
(Erschliessen Sie ganz
Südamerika mit Air France).
Teil einer Serie zur Förderung
des Air France Flugnetzes.
Öl und Acryl.

Artist/Artiste/Künstler
Jean Luc Falque
Art Director/Directeur
Artistique
Marc Gaillard
Copywriter/Rédacteur/Texter
Thierry Colignon
Advertising Agency/Agence de
Publicité/Werbeagentur
Havas Conseil
Client/Auftraggeber
Air France
Magazine advertisement,
"Gagnez l'Amérique avec Air
France." (Reach America with
Air France). Part of a series of
advertisements to promote the
Air France network.
Airbrush.
Publicité de revue, "Gagnez
l'Amérique avec Air France."
Partie d'une campagne de
publicité au profit du réseau
Air France.
Aérographe.
Zeitschriftenwerbung,
"Gagnez l'Amérique avec Air
France" (Erobern Sie Amerika
mit Air France). Teil einer
Serie zur Förderung des Air
France Flugnetzes.
Spritztechnik.

Artist/Artiste/Künstler
Michel Dubré
Art Director/Directeur
Artistique
John Scott
Copywriter/Rédacteur/Texter
Françoise Delafosse
Advertising Agency/Agence de
Publicité/Werbeagentur
De Plas Homsy Delafosse
Client/Auftraggeber
Champagne Mercier
Press advertisement for
Champagne Mercier, "Il y a
toujours eu un brin de folie
dans notre champagne" (There
has always been a little madness
in our champagne). Water-
colour and engraving, in colour.
Publicité de presse pour le
Champagne Mercier, "Il y a
toujours eu un brin de folie dans
notre champagne." Aquarelle et
gravure, en couleurs.
Pressewerbung für Champagne
Mercier, "Il y a toujours eu un
brin de folie dans notre
champagne" (Unser
Champagner hat immer ein
bisschen Verrücktheit in sich
gehabt). Wasserfarben und
Gravur, farbig.

Artist/Artiste/Künstler
Paul Sample
Designer/Maquettiste/Gestalter
Mike Preston
Art Director/Directeur
Artistique
Mike Preston
Copywriter/Rédacteur/Texter
John Bailey
Advertising Agency/Agence de
Publicité/Werbeagentur
**J Walter Thompson
Company Limited**
Client/Auftraggeber
Pan American World Airways
Trade press advertisement,
which appeared in the 'Travel
Trade Gazette', "Pamper your
client. Book him on our First
Class Dining Room."
Pen and ink, in colour.
Publicité de presse
commerciale, parue dans la
'Travel Trade Gazette,' "Pamper
your client. Book him on our
First Class Dining Room."
(Choyez votre client. Faites-lui
une réservation dans notre
restaurant de première classe).
Plume et encre, en couleurs.
Fachzeitschriftenwerbung,
"Pamper your client. Book him
on our First Class Dining Room"
(Verwöhnen Sie Ihren Kunden.
Buchen Sie Ihn erster Klasse
in unseren Speisesalon),
erschienen in 'Travel Trade
Gazette'.
Feder und Tusche, farbig.

Artist/Artiste/Kunstler
Derek Benee
Designer/Maquettiste/Gestalter
Tom Bund
Art Director/Directeur
Artistique
Tom Bund
Advertising Agency/Agence de
Publicité
**J Walter Thompson
Company Limited (Belgium)**
Client/Auftraggeber
Quaker Oats
Press advertisement for Poussi
Regal cat food.
Airbrush.
Publicité de presse pour
nourriture de chat Poussi Regal.
Aérographe.
Pressewerbung für Poussi Regal
Katzenfutter.
Spritztechnik.

Artist/Artiste/Künstler
Guy Gladwell
Designer/Maquettiste/Gestalter
John Hegarty
Art Director/Directeur
Artistique
John Hegarty
Copywriter/Rédacteur/Texter
Neil Patterson
Advertising Agency/Agence de
Publicité/Werbeagentur
TBWA Limited
Client/Auftraggeber
Newsweek International
Press advertisement to promote
'Newsweek's' Asian news
coverage, "How is China
managing without Mao?''
Oils.
Publicité de presse pour
souligner l'importance des
reportages asiatiques de
'Newsweek', "How is China
managing without Mao?"
(Comment la Chine se
débrouille-t-elle sans Mao?).
Huile.
Pressewerbung für die
Nachrichtenübersicht aus
Asien in 'Newsweek', "How is
China managing without Mao?"
(Wie kommt China ohne Mao
aus?).
Öl.

Artist/Artiste/Künstler
Wayne Anderson
Art Director/Directeur
Artistique
Tony Muranka
Copywriter/Rédacteur/ Texter
Ken Mullen
Advertising Agency/Agence de
Publicité/Werbeagentur
**J Walter Thompson Company
Limited**
Client/Auftraggeber
Hedges & Butler Limited
Magazine advertisement, "It's
about as likely as a duff bottle of
Hirondelle", to illustrate the
phrase "Castles in the air",
Ink, crayon and pencil, in
colour.
Publicité de revue "It's about as
likely as a duff bottle of
Hirondelle" (C'est aussi
vraisemblable qu'une bouteille
d'Hirondelle altérée), pour
illustrer la phrase "Castle in the
air" (Chateaux en Espagne).
Encre, crayon de pastel et crayon,
en couleurs.
Zeitschriftenwerbung, "It's
about as likely as a duff bottle
of Hirondelle" (Es ist ungefähr
so wahrscheinlich wie eine
schlechte Flasche Hirondelle),
zur Redewendung "Castles in the
air" (Luftschlösser). Tusche,
Crayon und Bleistift, farbig.

Artist/Artiste/Künstler
Barry Craddock
Art Director/Directeur
Artistique
Tony Muranka
Copywriter/Rédacteur/Texter
Ken Mullen
Advertising Agency/Agence de
Publicité/Werbeagentur
**J Walter Thompson Company
Limited**
Client/Auftraggeber
Hedges & Butler Limited
Magazine advertisement, "It's
about as likely as a duff bottle of
Hirondelle", to illustrate the
phrase "Storm in a teacup",
Water-colour, in colour.
Publicité de revue "It's about as
likely as a duff bottle of
Hirondelle" (C'est aussi
vraisemblable qu'une bouteille
d'Hirondelle altérée) pour
illustrer la phrase "Storm in a
teacup" (Tempête dans une
tasse de thé) Aquarelle, en
couleurs.
Zeitschriftenwerbung, "It's about
as likely as a duff bottle of
Hirondelle" (Es ist ungefähr so
wahrscheinlich wie eine
schlechte Flasche Hirondelle),
zur Redewendung "Storm in a
teacup" (Sturm in der Teetasse).
Wasserfarben, farbig.

Artist/Artiste/Künstler
Will Rowlands
Designer/Maquettiste/Gestalter
Kevin Preston
Art Director/Directeur
Artistique
Kevin Preston
Advertising Agency/Agence de
Publicité/Werbeagentur
Royds (Manchester) Limited
Client/Auftraggeber
**Imperial Chemical Industries
Limited, Pharmaceuticals
Division**
Mailing shot to doctors called
"Angina and Cold". Part of a series
featuring the same man.
Airbrush and acrylics.
Envoi postal aux médecins
intitulé "Angina and Cold"
(L'angine et le froid). Partie d'une
série montrant le même homme.
Aérographe et acrylique.
Direktwerbung an Ärzte zum
Thema "Angina and Cold"
(Angina und Kälte). Teil einer
Serie mit derselben Hauptfigur.
Spritztechnik und Acryl.

Artist/Artiste/Künstler
Willi Rieser
Designer/Maquettiste/Gestalter
Susi Richli
Art Director/Directeur
Artistique
Helmut Rottke
Copywriter/Rédacteur/Texter
Bernd Arnold
Advertising Agency/Agence de
Publicité/Werbeagentur
GGK Düsseldorf
Client/Auftraggeber
Bundespost
Magazine advertisement.
Gouache, in colour.
Publicité de revue.
Gouache, en couleurs.
Zeitschriftenwerbung.
Gouache, farbig.

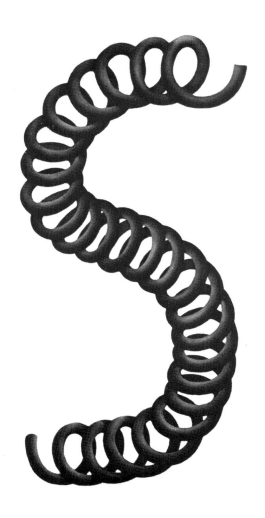

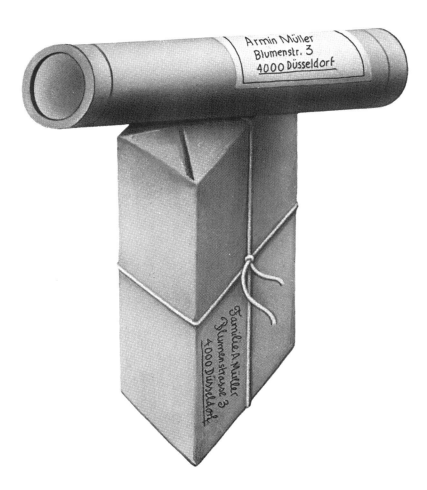

Armin Müller
Blumenstr. 3
4000 Düsseldorf

Familie A Müller
Blumenstrasse 3
4000 Düsseldorf

Artist/Artiste/Künstler
Christian Broutin
Art Director/Directeur
Artistique
Gérard Monot
Advertising Agency/Agence de
Publicité/Werbeagentur
TBWA
Client/Auftraggeber
**Philip Morris Societé
Anonyme**
Newspaper advertisement for
Philip Morris Filter Kings
using three consecutive pages.
Pen and ink.
Publicité de journal pour
Philip Morris Filter Kings
utilisant trois pages
consécutives.
Plume et encre.
Zeitungswerbung für Philip
Morris Filter Kings auf drei
Folgeseiten.
Feder und Tusche.

Artist/Artiste/Künstler
Philippe Caron
Art Director/Directeur
Artistique
Daniel Malissen
Advertising Agency/Agence de
Publicité/Werbeagentur
HMMA
Client/Auftraggeber
SEITA
Press advertisement for
Gauloises cigarettes. Crayon.
Publicité de presse pour les
cigarettes Gauloises. Crayon.
Pressewerbung für Gauloises
Zigaretten. Farbstifte.

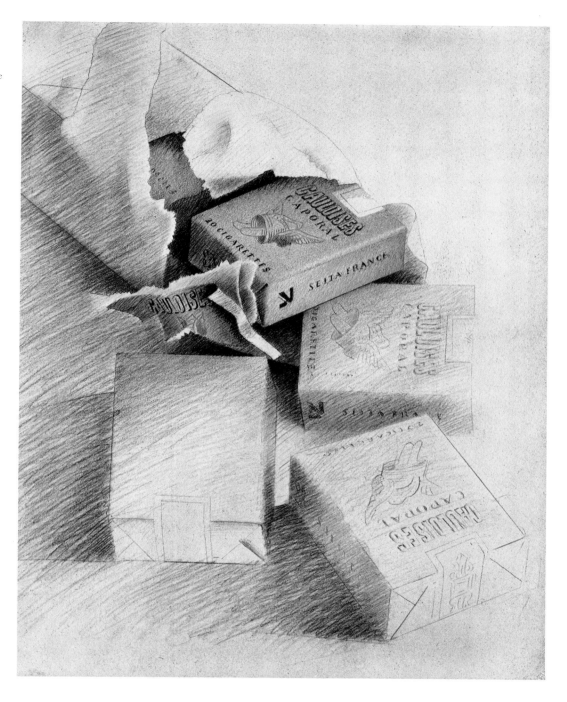

Posters
This section includes
work commissioned for
posters and prints.

Affiches
Cette section comprend
des travaux commandés
pour des affiches et des
imprimés.

Plakate
Dieser Abschnitt umfasst
Illustrationen für
Aussenwerbung und
Plakate.

Artist/Artiste/Künstler
Mike Golding
Designer/Maquettiste/Gestalter
Keith McEwan
Art Directors/Directeurs
Artistiques
Mike Golding
Keith McEwan
Client/Auftraggeber
Hij Herenmode
"Kÿk Hÿ nou," poster advertising men's leisure wear.
Acrylic.
"Kÿk Hÿ nou," affiche de publicité pour la mode masculine de loisir. Acrylique.
"Kÿk Hÿ nou," Werbeposter für Freizeitkleidung für Herren.
Acryl.

Artist/Artiste/Künstler
Mike Golding
Designer/Maquettiste/Gestalter
Keith McEwan
Art Directors/Directeurs
Artistiques
Mike Golding
Keith McEwan
Client/Auftraggeber
Hij Herenmode
"Kÿk Hÿ nou," poster advertising men's wear. Acrylic.
"Kÿk Hÿ nou," affiche de publicité de mode masculine. Acrylique.
"Kÿk Hÿ nou," Werbeposter für Herrenbekleidung. Acryl.

179

Artist/Artiste/Künstler
Guy Billout
Art Director/Directeur
Artistique
Carol Carson
Copywriter/Rédacteur/Texter
Jean Marzollo
Client/Auftraggeber
Scholastic Magazines
Educational poster for 'Let's
Find Out', "What's wrong here?"
Water-colour, in colour.
Affiche pédogogique pour 'Let's
Find Out', "What's wrong here?"
(Qu'est-ce qui ne va pas ici?).
Aquarelle, en couleurs.
Schulungs-Poster für 'Let's Find
Out', "What's wrong here?"
(Was ist hier falsch?). Wasser-
farben, farbig.

Artist/Artiste/Künstler
Hergé
Art Director/Directeur
Artistique
Jean-Luc Collard
Copywriter/Rédacteur/Texter
Serge Nallot
Advertising Agency/Agence de
Publicité/Werbeagentur
Havas-Conseil
Client/Auftraggeber
Agio Mehari's
Poster for Mehari's small cigars,
"Agio Mehari's. Le cigare des
Jeunes jusqu' à 77 ans' (Agio
Mehari's. The cigar for young
people up to the age of 77.).
Gouache, en couleur.
Affiche pour les petits cigares –
Mehari's, "Agio Mehari's. Le
cigare des Jeunes jusqu'à 77 ans.'
Gouache, en couleurs.
Poster für Mehari's Zigarillos,
"Agio Mehari's. Le cigare des
Jeunes jusqu' à 77 ans" (Agio
Mehari's. Die Zigarre für junge
Leute bis 77 Jahre). Gouache,
farbig.

Artist/Artiste/Künstler
Barry Trengrove
Client/Auftraggeber
Taramina Fashions
Poster for a fashion house,
showing fabrics and colour
themes but not specific clothes
styles. Water-colour, pencil
and collage.
Affiche pour une maison de
haute-couture, montrant des
tissus et des thèmes de coloris
mais pas de modes spécifiques.
Aquarelle, crayon et collage.
Poster für ein Modehaus, das
Stoffe und Farbmuster, aber
keinen bestimmten Kleidungs-
stil zeigt. Wasserfarben, Bleistift
und Collage.

Artist/Artiste/Künstler
Helmut Rottke
Designer/Maquettiste/Gestalter
Susi Richli
Art Director/Directeur
Artistique
Helmut Rottke
Copywriter/Rédacteur/Texter
Bernd Arnold
Advertising Agency/Agence de
Publicité/Werbeagentur
GGK
Client/Auftraggeber
Bundespost

Poster appearing in Post Offices,
"Telefonieren ist schön" (It's
nice to telephone!). Pens, in
colour.
Une affiche qu'on voit dans les
bureaux de poste: "Telefonieren
ist schön" (C'est bien de télé-
phoner). Plumes, en couleurs.
Poster für Postämter, "Telefonieren ist schön." Farbige
Stifte.

Artist/Artiste/Künstler
Glynn Boyd Harte
Designer/Maquettiste/Gestalter
Glynn Boyd Harte
Client/Auftraggeber
The Thumb Gallery
Poster for exhibition of the
artist's own work. Coloured
pencil.
Affiche pour une exposition du
travail de l'artiste. Crayon de
couleur.
Poster für eine Ausstellung des
Künstlers. Farbstifte.

185

Artist/Artiste/Künstler
Jean-Luc Falque
Art Director/Directeur
Artistique
Anne Falque
Client/Auftraggeber
Lancôme
Poster for the 1978 Lancôme
Golf Trophy. Airbrush, in
colour.
Affiche pour le trophée de Golf
Lancôme 1978. Aérographe, en
couleurs.
Poster für die Lancôme Golf
Trophäe 1978. Spritztechnik,
farbig.

Artist/Artiste/Künstler
Paul Leith
Art Director/Directeur
Artistique
Bernard Bureau
Advertising Agency/Agence de
Publicité/Werbeagentur
Ogilvy & Mather, Paris
Client/Auftraggeber
Mercedes Benz, France
Poster for a golf tournament
sponsored by Mercedes Benz.
Coloured pencils.
Affiche pour un tournoi de golf
subventionné par Mercedes
Benz. Crayons de couleurs.
Poster für ein Golftournier
gefördert von Mercedes Benz.
Farbstifte.

Artist/Artiste/Künstler
Keith McEwan
Designer/Maquettiste/Gestalter
Keith McEwan
Art Directors/Directeurs
Artistique
Lex de Rooy
Keith McEwan
Client/Auftraggeber
Eurofashion, Amsterdam
Poster advertising Madras
cotton clothing for men, pro-
jecting the idea of eastern cloths
coming west. Acrylic, in colour.
Affiche de publicité pour les
vêtements d'homme en coton
Madras, lançant l'idée de faire
venir les vêtements orientaux
vers l'ouest. Acrylique, en
couleurs.
Werbeposter für Herren-
bekleidung aus Madras
Baumwolle, zur Förderung von
orientalischen Stoffen im
Westen. Acryl, farbig.

Artist/Artiste/Künstler
Gabriel Pascalini
Designer/Maquettiste/Gestalter
Serge Simon
Copywriter/Rédacteur/Texter
Isabelle Leconte
Advertising Agency/Agence de
Publicité/Werbeagentur.
Young & Rubicam
Client/Auftraggeber
Kronenbourg BSN
Illustration (after Bonnard)
portraying the good times,
"Kronenbourg tant qu'il y aura
de bons moments" (Kronen-
bourg, as long as there are good
times). Oils, in colour.
Illustration (d'après Bonnard)
décrivant le bon temps,
"Kronenbourg tant qu'il y aura
de bons moments." Huile, en
couleurs.
Illustration (nach Bonnard)
über die guten Zeiten,
"Kronenbourg tant qu'il y aura
de bons moments" (So viele
Kronenbourgs wie es gute
Zeiten gibt). Öl, farbig.

Artist/Artiste/Künstler
Hector Cattolica
Client/Auftraggeber
Los Indianos
Poster for Los Indianos, a group
of Argentinian dancers, for
whom the artist was asked to
create a graphic impression of
their dances. "Choreographic
Visions of South America."
Acrylic.
Affiche pour Los Indianos,
groupe de danseurs argentins,
pour qui on a demandé à l'artiste
de créer une impression
graphique de leurs danses.
"Choreographic Visions of
South America" (Visions
chorégraphiques d'Amérique du
Sud). Acrylique.
Poster für Los Indianos, eine
Gruppe argentinischer Tänzer,
für die der Künstler eine
grafische Impression ihrer
Tänze gestaltete. "Choreographic
Visions of South America"
(Choreografische Bilder
Südamerikas). Acryl.

Artist/Artiste/Künstler
Milton Glaser
Art Director/Directeur
Artistique
Giorgio Soavi
Client/Auftraggeber
Ing C Olivetti & C SpA,
Poster for 'Lexicon 83', portable
electric typewriter. Gouache.
Affiche pour 'Lexicon 83',
machine à écrire portative
électrique. Gouache.
Poster für die 'Lexicon 83'
elektrische Reiseschreib-
maschine. Gouache.

Artist/Artiste/Künstler
Jacques Tardi
Art Director/Directeur
Artistique
Massin
Publisher/Editeur/Verlag
Editions Gallimard
Poster to promote the series of
detective books, Carré Noir,
"Carré Noir, tu connais?" (Do
you know Carré Noir?).
Gouache, in colour.
Affiche de publicité pour la
série Carré Noir de romans
policiers "Carré Noir, tu
connais?" Gouache, en couleurs.
Poster für eine Serie von Carré
Noir Detektivbüchern, "Carré
Noir, tu connais?" (Kennen Sie
Carré Noir?). Gouache, farbig.

Artist/Artiste/Künstler
Arthur Robins
Designer/Maquettiste/Gestalter
Paul Walter
Art Director/Directeur
Artistique
Paul Walter
Copywriter/Rédacteur/Texter
BBDO Copy Group
Advertising Agency/Agence de
Publisité/Werbeagentur
BBDO Limited
Client/Auftraggeber
Allied Breweries (UK) Limited
48 sheet poster for Skol lager,
"Skol drinking. It's the taste that
makes you do it." Black line with
water-colour, in colour.
Affiche à 48 feuilles pour la
bière Skol, "Skol drinking. It's
the taste that makes you do it."
(Boire de la Skol. C'est le goût
qui vous y pousse.) Ligne noire
et aquarelle, en couleurs.
48 Bogen Poster für Skol
Lagerbier, "Skol drinking. It's
the taste that makes you do it"
(Skol trinken. Der Geschmack
macht's aus). Schwarze Kontur-
linie und Wasserfarben, farbig.

Artist/Artiste/Künstler
Arthur Robins
Designer/Maquettiste/Gestalter
Paul Walter
Art Directors/Directeurs
Artistiques
Olavi Hakkinen
Paul Walter
Copywriter/Rédacteur/Texter
BBDO Copy Group
Advertising Agency/Agence de
Publicité/Werbeagentur
BBDO Limited
Client/Auftraggeber
Allied Breweries (UK) Limited
48 sheet poster for Skol lager,
"Skol drinking. It's the taste that
makes you do it." Black line with
water-colour.
Affiche à 48 feuilles pour la bière
Skol, "Skol drinking. It's the
taste that makes you do it." (Boire
de la Skol. C'est le goût qui vous
y pousse.) Ligne noire et
aquarelle.
48 Bogen Poster für Skol
Lagerbier, "Skol drinking. It's
the taste that makes you do it"
(Skol trinken. Der Geschmack
macht's aus). Schwarze Kontur-
linie und Wasserfarben.

Artist/Artiste/Künstler
Marina Langer-Rosa
Art Editor/Rédacteur
Artistique/Kunstredakteur
Theo Burauen
Art Director/Directeur
Artistique
Helmut Langer
Design Group/Groupe de
Graphistes/Design-Gruppe
Visualisation Langer
Client/Auftraggeber
Zoologischer Garten AG, Köln
Poster to promote Cologne Zoo,
"Der Kölner Zoo lädt ein"
(Cologne Zoo invites you to
visit). Water-colour, airbrush.
Affiche de promotion pour le
Zoo de Cologne "Der Kölner
Zoo lädt ein" (Le Zoo de
Cologne invite). Aquarelle,
aérographe.
Poster für den Kölner Zoo, "Der
Kölner Zoo lädt ein." Wasser-
farben und Spritztechnik,
farbig.

Artist/Artiste/Künstler
Stuart Bodek
Art Director/Directeur
Artistique
Wim Bartels
Advertising Agency/Agence de
Publicité/Werbeagentur
**Franzen Hey &
Veltman/BBDO**
Client/Auftraggeber
Amstel Bier
Poster for a fancy dress beer
festival showing six close-ups
of heads, all wearing carnival
noses. Acrylic, in colour.
Affiche pour un festival de la
bière en déguisé montrant six
gros-plans de têtes portant
toutes des nez de carnaval.
Acrylique, en couleurs.
Poster für ein kostümiertes
Bierfest mit Nahansichten von
sechs Köpfen mit Karnevalnasen.
Acryl, farbig.

Artist/Artiste/Künstler
Mick Brownfield
Art Director/Directeur
Artistique
Tony Kay
Advertising Agency/Agence de
Publicité/Werbeagentur
**Collett Dickenson Pearce &
Partners Limited**
Client/Auftraggeber
Whitbread & Company Limited
Poster for Heineken lager
featuring the footballer, Joe
Jordan, "Heineken refreshes
the parts other beers cannot
reach." Gouache and ink, in
colour.
Affiche pour la bière Heineken
montrant le footballer, Joe Jordan,
"Heineken refreshes the parts
other beers cannot reach."
(Heineken rafraîchit les endroits
que les autres bières ne peuvent
atteindre). Gouache et encre,
en couleurs.
Poster für Heineken Lagerbier
mit dem Fussballer Joe Jordan,
"Heineken refreshes the parts
other beers cannot reach"
(Heineken erfrischt die Teile,
die andere Biere gar nicht
erreichen). Gouache und Tusche,
farbig.

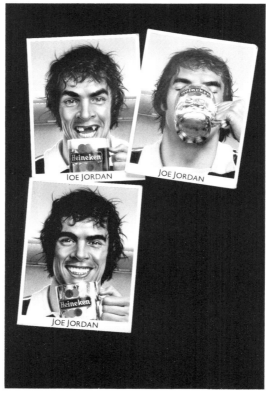

Artist/Artiste/Künstler
Alan Baker
Designer/Maquettiste/Gestalter
Ian Chambers
Art Director/Directeur
Artistique
Ian Chambers
Client/Auftraggeber
The Zip Art Company Limited
Self-promotional poster for the
artist. One from a series of
drawings on an ecological
theme. Gouache.
Affiche publicitaire pour
l'artiste. L'un d'une série de
dessins à thème écologique.
Gouache.
Eigenwerbungsposter des
Künstlers innerhalb einer Serie
von Zeichnungen über
ecologische Themen. Gouache.

Artist/Artiste/Künstler
Larry Learmonth
Designer/Maquettiste/Gestalter
Larry Learmonth
Client/Auftraggeber
Studio 10
Poster designed as Christmas
gift from Studio 10. Oils on
canvas.
Affiche destinée à être un cadeau
de Noël du Studio 10. Huile sur
toile.
Poster verwendet als Weihnachts-
geschenk vom Studio 10.
Öl auf Leinwand.

Artist/Artiste/Künstler
Guy Billout
Art Director/Directeur
Artistique
Deborah Lyn Thomas
Client/Auftraggeber
WBAI
Poster for the Sixth Annual
WBAI Holiday Craft Fair, held
in Columbia, USA. Water-colour,
in colour.
Affiche de la sixième foire
annuelle des WBAI Holiday
Craft, tenue au Columbia, États-
Unis d'Amérique. Aquarelle,
en couleurs.
Poster für die sechste jährliche
WBAI Holiday Craft Fair in
Columbia, USA. Wasserfarben,
farbig.

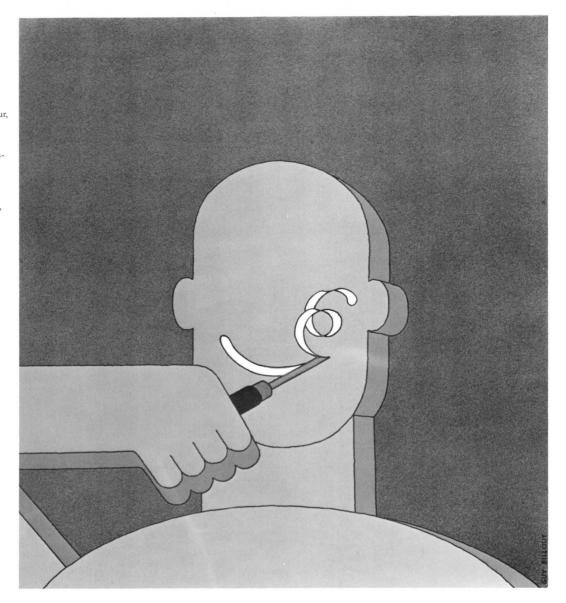

Artist/Artiste/Künstler
Brian Grimwood
Designer/Maquettiste/Gestalter
Brian Grimwood
Client/Auftraggeber
Cream Studio
Christmas card promotion, "It's
not just at Christmas we make
your eyes flutter." Gouache, in
colour.
Promotion de cartes de Noël,
It's not just at Christmas we
make your eyes flutter." (Ce n'est
pas qu' à Noël que nous vous
éblouissons) Gouache, en
couleurs.
Werbende Weihnachtskarte,
"It's not just at Christmas we
make your eyes flutter" (Wir
bringen Aufregung nicht nur
um die Weihnachtszeit).
Gouache, farbig.

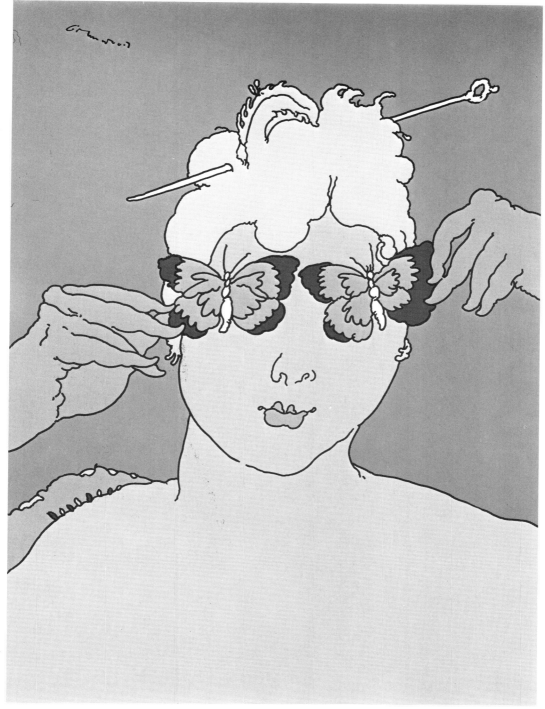

Artist/Artiste/Künstler
Seymour Chwast
Art Director/Directeur
Artistique
Jean Charles Salaun
Copywriter/Rédacteur/Texter
Anne Marie Flamand-Kellal
Advertising Agency/Agence de
Publicité/Werbeagentur
Havas Conseil
Client /Auftraggeber
**Caisse Nationale de
Crédit Agricole**
Poster to promote the Crédit
Agricole, "Simplifiez-vous la
vie" (Simplify your life). One of
a series of decorative posters to
create a less formal image for
the bank. Collage.
Affiche pour la promotion du
Crédit Agricole "Simplifiez-
vous la vie." L'une d'une série
d'affiches destinées à établir une
image moins conventionnelle
de la Banque. Collage.
Poster für die Crédit Agricole,
"Simplifiez-vous la vie"
(Machen Sie sich Ihr Leben
einfacher), innerhalb einer
Serie dekorativer Poster zur
Förderung eines weniger
formellen Images für die Bank.
Collage.

Artist/Artiste/Künstler
Milton Glaser
Art Director/Directeur
Artistique
Jean Charles Salaun
Copywriter/Rédacteur/Texter
Anne Marie Flamand-Kellal
Advertising Agency/Agence de
Publicité/Werbeagentur
Havas Conseil
Client/Auftraggeber
**Caisse Nationale de
Crédit Agricole**
Poster to promote the Credit
Agricole, "Vos intérêts
s'annoncent bien" (Your interests
are in good hands). One of a
series of decorative posters to
create a less formal image for
the bank. Inks and transfers.
Affiche de promotion du Crédit
Agricole, "Vos intérêts
s'annoncent bien." L'une d'une
série d'affiches décoratives
destinées à établir une image
moins conventionnelle de la
banque. Encres et décal-
comanies.
Poster für die Crédit Agricole,
"Vos intérêts s'annoncent bien"
(Ihre Interessen sind in guten
Händen), innerhalb einer Serie
dekorativer Poster zur Förderung
eines weniger formellen Images
für die Bank. Tusche und
Umdruck.

Artist/Artiste/Künstler
Etienne Delessert
Art Director/Directeur
Artistique
Jean Charles Salaun
Copywriter/Rédacteur/Texter
Anne Marie Flamand-Kellal
Advertising Agency/Agence de
Publicité/Werbeagentur
Havas Conseil
Client/Auftraggeber
**Caisse Nationale de
Crédit Agricole**
Poster to promote the Crédit
Agricole, "Améliorez votre
retraite" (Improve your retire-
ment). One of a series of decor-
ative posters to create a less
formal image for the bank.
Crayon.
Affiche pour la promotion du
Crédit Agricole, "Améliorez
votre retraite." L'une d'une série
d'affiches décoratives destinées
à établir une image moins
conventionnelle de la banque.
Crayon de pastel.
Poster für die Crédit Agricole,
"Améliorez votre retraite"
(Geniessen Sie Ihren
Ruhestand), innerhalb einer
Serie dekorativer Poster zur
Förderung eines weniger
formellen Images für die Bank.
Crayon.

Artist/Artiste/Künstler
Alain Le Foll
Art Director/Directeur
Artistique
Jean Charles Salaun
Copywriter/Rédacteur/Texter
Anne Marie Flamand-Kellal
Advertising Agency/Agence de
Publicité/Werbeagentur
Havas Conseil
Client/Auftraggeber
**Caisse Nationale de
Crédit Agricole**
Poster to promote the Crédit
Agricole, "Installez vous con-
fortablement" (Make yourself
comfortable). One of a series of
decorative posters to create a
less formal image for the bank.
Pastels and water-colour.
Affiche de promotion du Crédit
Agricole "Installez vous con-
fortablement." L'une d'une série
d'affiches décoratives destinées
à établir une image moins con-
ventionnelle de la Banque.
Pastels et aquarelle.
Poster für die Crédit Agricole,
"Installez vous confortable-
ment" (Machen Sie es sich
gemütlich), innerhalb einer
Serie dekorativer Poster zur
Förderung eines weniger
formellen Images für die Bank.
Pastell- und Wasserfarben.

Artist/Artiste/Künstler
André François
Art Director/Directeur
Artistique
Jean Charles Salaun
Copywriter/Rédacteur/Texter
Anne Marie Flamand-Kellal
Advertising Agency/Agence de
Publicité/Werbeagentur
Havas Conseil
Client/Auftraggeber
**Caisse Nationale de
Crédit Agricole**
Poster to promote the Crédit
Agricole's housing loan scheme,
"C'est si bon d'être chez soi"
(It's so good to be at home). One
of a series of decorative posters
to create a less formal image for
the bank. Pastel ink and water-
colour.
Affiche pour la promotion du
plan de prêt logement du Crédit
Agricole "C'est si bon d'être
chez soi." L'une d'une série
d'affiches décoratives destinée
à établir une image moins
conventionnelle de la banque.
Encre pastel et aquarelle.
Poster für den Hausdarlehen-
Plan der Crédit Agricole, "C'est
si bon d'être chez soi" (Es ist so
schön, zu Hause zu sein),
innerhalb einer Serie dekorativer
Poster zur Förderung eines
weniger formellen Images für
die Bank. Pastelltusche und
Wasserfarben.

Artist/Artiste/Künstler
Jan Mlodozeniec
Art Director/Directeur
Artistique
Krystyna Töpfer
Publisher/Editeur/Verlag
Iskry
Poster to mark the 25th anniversary of the publishing house Iskry, which specialises in children's books. Gouache, in colour.
Affiche marquant le 25e anniversaire de la maison d'édition Iskry, qui se spécialise en livres d'enfants. Gouache, en couleurs.
Poster zum Anlass des 25-jährigen Jubiläums des Verlagshauses Iskry, das sich auf Kinderbücher spezialisiert. Gouache, farbig.

Artist/Artiste/Künstler
Jan Mlodozeniec
Art Director/Directeur
Artistique
Tadeusz Jodlowski
Client/Auftraggeber
**Krajewa Agencja
Wydawnicza**
Decorative poster.
Gouache, in colour.
Affiche décorative.
Gouache, en couleurs.
Dekoratives Poster.
Gouache, farbig.

Artist/Artiste/Künstler
H P Kunkel
Art Director/Directeur
Artistique
Uli Weber
Copywriter/Rédacteur/Texter
Brigitte Fussnegger
Advertising Agency/Agence de
Publicité/Werbeagentur
Leonhardt & Kern
Client/Auftraggeber
Mustang Künzelsau
Poster for Mustang jeans,
"Don't forget your Mustangs."
Oils.
Affiche pour les jeans Mustang,
"Don't forget your Mustangs"
(N'oublie pas ton Mustang).
Huile.
Poster für Mustang Jeans,
"Don't forget your Mustangs"
(Ihre Mustangs nicht vergessen).
Öl.

Artist/Artiste/Künstler
H P Kunkel
Art Director/Directeur
Artistique
Uli Weber
Advertising Agency/Agence de
Publicité/Werbeagentur
Leonhardt & Kern
Client/Auftraggeber
Mustang Künzelsau
Poster for Mustang jeans.
Oils.
Affiche pour les jeans Mustang.
Huile.
Poster für Mustang Jeans.
Öl.

Design
This section includes
work commissioned for
calendars, diaries, direct
mail announcements,
greetings cards, pack-
aging, promotional
booklets, promotional
mailings, record sleeves,
stationery, technical and
industrial catalogues.

Design
Cette section comprend
des travaux commandés
pour les calendriers,
agendas, lettres circulaires,
cartes des voeux,
emballages, livrets de
promotion, promotion
par poste, pochettes de
disques, papeterie, cata-
logues techniques et
industriels.

Gebrauchsgraphik
Dieser Abschnitt umfasst
Arbeiten für Agenden,
Kalender, Werbeaus-
sendungen, Grusskarten,
Verpackungsartikel,
Prospekte, Schallplatten-
hüllen, Briefköpfe,
Technische und
Industriekataloge.

Artist/Artiste/Künstler
Bruno K Wiese
Designer/Maquettiste/Gestalter
Bruno K Wiese
Client/Auftraggeber
**United Nations Postal
Administration**
Stamp design for United Nations,
"Combat Racism". The design
first appeared in 'Form'
magazine in 1977 and has been
awarded first prize in a world-
wide design competition. The
stamp was placed on sale in the
USA in September 1977.
Airbrush and water-colour,
in colour.
Timbre pour les Nations Unies,
"Combat Racism" (Combattez
le racisme). La maquette a
d'abord été présentée en 1977
dans la revue 'Form' et a reçu le
premier prix d'un concours
mondial de design. Le timbre
a été mis en vente aux Etats Unis
en septembre 1977. Aérographe
et aquarelle, en couleurs.
Briefmarke für die United
Nations "Combat Racism"
(Kämpfen Sie gegen den
Rassismus). Das Design erschien
ursprünglich in der Zeitschrift
'Form' im Jahre 1977 und erhielt
den ersten Preis in einem
weltweiten Design-Wettbewerb.
Die Briefmarke wird seit
September 1977 in den USA
verkauft. Wasserfarben und
Spritztechnik, farbig.

Artist/Artiste/Künstler
René van Raalte
Designer/Maquettiste/Gestalter
René van Raalte
Client/Auftraggeber
**Staatsbedrijf Der
Posterijen, Telegrafie
en Telefonie**
Child Welfare Stamps issued
15th November 1977. The stamps
show different areas of risk of
accidents to children in and
around the home. Water-colour
and airbrush.
Timbres de protection de
l'enfance émis le 15 novembre
1977. Les timbres montrent les
différents secteurs de risques
d'accidents aux enfants à la
maison. Aquarelle et aérographe.
Kinderwohlfahrtsmarken,
erschienen am 15. November
1977. Die Marken zeigen verschiedene Bereiche im und um das
Heim, wo das Risiko von
Unfällen für Kinder gross ist.
Wasserfarben und Spritztechnik.

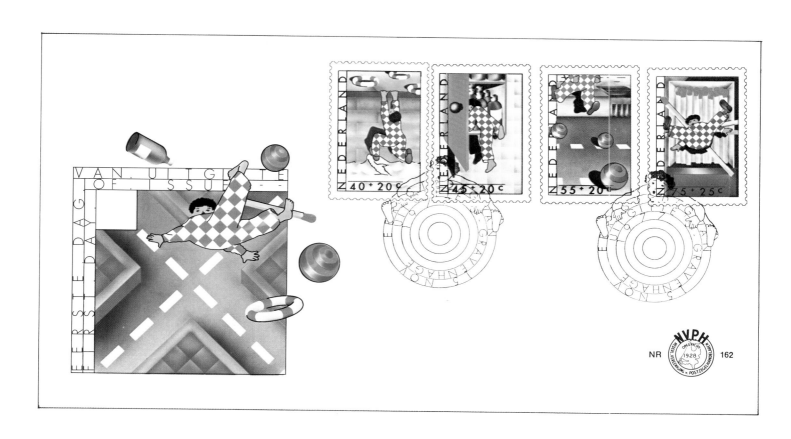

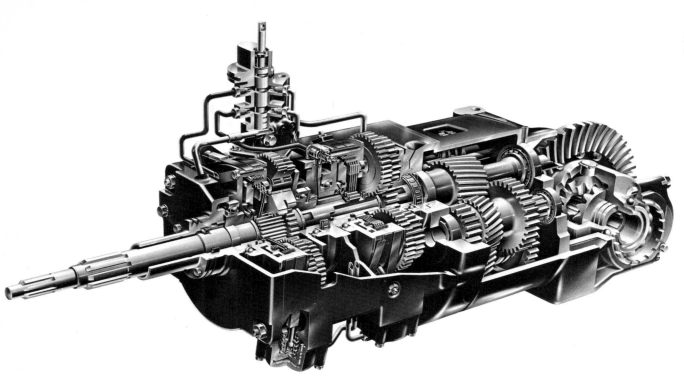

Artist/Artiste/Künstler
Tom Liddell
Designer/Maquettiste/Gestalter
Gordon Halls
Art Director/Directeur
Artistique
Neil Schofield
Client/Auftraggeber
**David Brown Tractors Limited,
Huddersfield**
Wallchart for the DB 1212 Hydra-
shift semi-automatic gearbox.
Full colour illustration from a
pencil drawing by Terry
Palfreyman. Gouache, in colour.
Carte murale de la boite de
vitesse semi-automatique Hydra-
shift DB 1212. Illustration en
couleurs à partir d'un dessin au
crayon par Terry Palfreyman.
Gouache, en couleurs.
Wandkarte für das DB 1212
Hydra-verstellbar semi-
automatische Getriebe. Farbige
Illustration nach einer Bleistift-
zeichnung von Terry Palfreyman.
Gouache, farbig.

Artist/Artiste/Künstler
Alan Fisher
Art Director/Directeur
Artistique
Geoff Dean
Advertising Agency/Agence de
Publicité/Werbeagentur
Reid Walker Limited
Client/Auftraggeber
Fiat Motor Company Limited
Press advertisement.
Scraperboard, in black and
white.
Publicité de presse.
Ripage, en noir et blanc.
Pressewerbung.
Schabtechnik, schwarzweiss.

Artist/Artiste/Künstler
John Verberk
Art Director/Directeur
Artistique
Ruud Hoek
Advertising Agency/Agence de
Publicité/Werbeagentur
Advertising Art Centre
Client/Auftraggeber
Amro-Bank
A free interpretation of a day in
the bank, illustration for the
annual report of the Amro-Bank.
Gouache.
Interprétation libre d'une
journée à la banque. Illustration
pour le rapport annuel de la
Amro-Bank. Gouache.
Eine freie Interpretation eines
Tages im Bankwesen. Illustration
für den Jahresbericht der
Amro-Bank. Gouache.

Artist/Artiste/Künstler
Gerlinde Mader
Art Director/Directeur
Artistique
Gerlinde Mader
Publisher/Editeur/Verlag
Maders Grafik Design
Christmas and New Year card.
Water-colour.
Carte de Noël et de Nouvel An.
Aquarelle.
Weihnachts- und Neujahrskarte.
Wasserfarben.

Artist/Artiste/Künstler
Martin White
Designer/Maquettiste/Gestalter
Martin White
Publisher/Editeur/Verlag
Pictures
Small card illustrating the verse
"The frail are pressed to the rail."
Pencil and pencil crayon, in
colour.
Petite carte illustrant le vers
"The frail are pressed to the rail"
(Les faibles sont poussés sur
les barrières). Crayon et pastel
mine, en couleurs.
Kärtchen zur Illustration des
Verses "The frail are pressed to
the rail" (Die Schwachen werden
gegen das Gitter gedrängt).
Bleistift und Crayon, farbig.

Artist/Artiste/Künstler
Sara Midda
Art Director/Directeur
Artistique
Jan Pienkowski
Publisher/Editeur/Verlag
Gallery Five
Six Christmas cards.
Water-colour, in colour.
Six cartes de Noël.
Aquarelle, en couleurs.
Sechs Weihnachtskarten.
Wasserfarben, farbig.

Artist/Artiste/Künstler
Chloe Cheese
Designer/Maquettiste/Gestalter
Alan McDougal
Art Director/Directeur
Artistique
Stafford Cliff
Publisher/Editeur/Verlag
Conran Associates Limited
Illustrations for 'Cook's Diary'
(L'agenda de la cuisinière)
by Cynthia Wickham with an
illustrated recipe for each week
of 1979. Pencil, crayon and
water-colour.
Illustrations pour 'Cook's Diary'
par Cynthia Wickham avec une
recette illustrée pour chaque
semaine de 1979. Crayon, crayon
de pastel et aquarelle.
Illustrationen für das 'Cook's
Diary' (Koch-Kalender) von
Cynthia Wickham, mit einem
illustrierten Rezept für jede
Woche des Jahres 1979.
Bleistift, Crayon und
Wasserfarben.

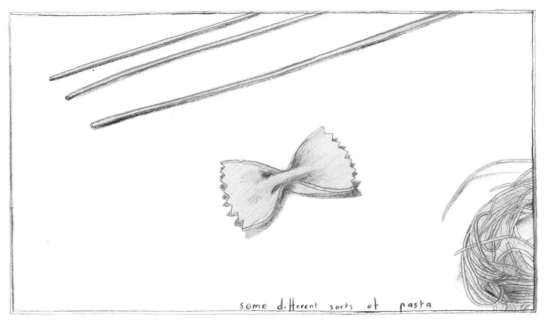

some different sorts of pasta

Artist/Artiste/Künstler
Michael Lunt
Designer/Maquettiste/Gestalter
Michael Lunt
Client/Auftraggeber
Roadstone Limited
Illustration of The Maltings,
Cork, for the Roadstone
Calendar. The calendar was
designed to show aspects of
Irish architecture, particularly
buildings of merit normally
overlooked. Acrylic, in colour.
Illustration de The Maltings,
Cork, pour le calendrier de
Roadstone. Le calendrier a été
conçu pour montrer des aspects
de l'architecture irlandaise, en
particulier de bâtiments de
valeur souvent ignorés.
Acrylique, en couleurs.
Illustration der Maltings in Cork
für den Roadstone Kalender. Der
Kalender zeigt Aspekte irischer
Architektur, insbesondere
markante Gebäude, die
normalerweise übersehen
werden. Acrylfarbe, farbig.

Artist/Artiste/Künstler
Christian Desbois
Art Editor/Rédacteur
Artistique/Kunstredakteur
Marc Combier
Publisher/Editeur/Verlag
Marc Combier Communications
Postcard from 'La Collection
des Illustrateurs 1977', showing
two tramps asleep beneath a
seaside poster. "A chacun son
coin de Paradis" (Each has his
corner of Paradise). Oils.
Carte postale de 'La Collection
des Illustrateurs 1977', montrant
deux chemineaux endormis
sous une affiche de station
balnéaire "A chacun son coin
de Paradis." Huile.
Postkarte aus der 'Collection
des Illustrateurs 1977', die zwei
schlafende Landstreicher unter
einem Palmküsten-Poster zeigt.
"A chacun son coin de Paradis"
(Jeder hat seine eigene Ecke
im Paradies). Öl.

Artist/Artiste/Künstler
Pierre Peyrolle
Art Editor/Rédacteur
Artistique/Kunstredakteur
Marcel Germon
Art Director/Directeur
Artistique
Alain Anseau
Advertising Agency/Agence de
Publicité/Werbeagentur
Agence Marcel Germon
Client/Auftraggeber
Mobilier de France
Cover for furniture catalogue.
Oils.
Couverture de catalogue de
mobilier. Huile.
Umschlag für einen Möbel-
katalog. Öl.

Artist/Artiste/Künstler
Pierre Le-Tan
Art Editor/Rédacteur
Artistique/Kunstredakteur
Carol Southern
Publisher/Editeur/Verlag
Clarkson N Potter Incorporated
Invitation for an exhibition at
the Gotham Book Mart gallery,
New York, November 1977.
Pen, ink and wash, in black
and white.
Invitation à une exposition à la
Gotham Book Mart gallery,
New York, novembre 1977.
Plume, encre et lavis, en noir
et blanc.
Einladung für eine Ausstellung
in der Gotham Book Mart
Gallerie, New York, November
1977. Feder und Tusche,
laviert, schwarzweiss.

Artist/Artiste/Künstler
Jean Marie Renard

The March page from the Royal
College of Art's end of term
calendar. "March comes in like
a lion and goes out like a lamb."
Water-colour, in colour.
La page pour mars du calendrier
de fin de trimestre du Royal
College of Art. "March comes in
like a lion and goes out like a
lamb" (Le mois de mars arrive
comme un lion et repart comme
un agneau). Aquarelle, en
couleurs.
Die März-Seite des Royal College
of Art Kalenders zum Semester-
abschluss. "March comes in like
a lion and goes out like a lamb"
(Der März kündet sich an wie
ein Löwe und geht aus wie ein
Lamm). Wasserfarben, farbig.

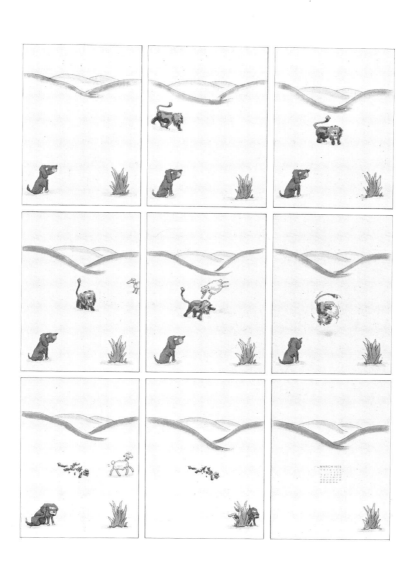

Artist/Artiste/Künstler
Peter Brookes
Designer/Maquettiste/Gestalter
Peter Brookes
Art Director/Directeur
Artistique
Peter Windett
Design Group/Groupe de
Graphistes/Design-Gruppe
Peter Windett Associates
Client/Auftraggeber
Crabtree & Evelyn Limited

Tin for Crabtree & Evelyn
Country Biscuits from the
Yorkshire Dales. Illustrations
for top and sides of the tin, the
mediaeval designs reflecting
the hand-made product.
Gouache.
Boite pour Crabtree & Evelyn
Country Biscuits from the
Yorkshire Dales. Illustrations
pour le haut et les côtés de la
boite, les dessins médiévaux
reflétant le produit fait à la main.
Gouache.
Dose für Crabtree & Evelyn
Kekse aus den Yorkshire Dales.
Illustrationen für Deckel und
Seiten der Dose, die mittel-
alterlich in Gestaltung und die
handgemachte Qualität des
Produkts reflektieren sollten.
Gouache.

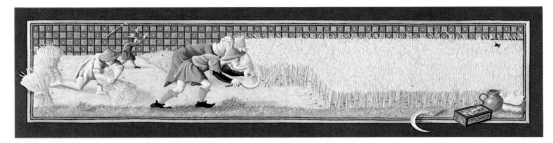

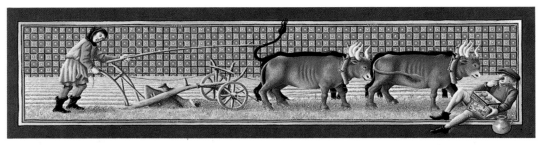

Artist/Artiste/Künstler
Jean Claude Lutton
Art Director/Directeur
Artistique
Jean-Marie Heno
Advertising Agency/Agence de
Publicité/Werbeagentur
**Crehalet Foliot Robert
& Partners**
Illustration to be published in
'La Banque'.
Water-colour and ink.
Illustration qui sera publiée
dans 'La Banque'.
Aquarelle et encre.
Illustration zur Veröffentlichung
in 'La Banque'. Wasserfarben
und Tusche.

Artist/Artiste/Künstler
Mike Noomé
Designers/Maquettistes/
Gestalter
Colin Craig
David Druiff
Art Director/Directeur
Artistique
Peter Wagg
Client/Auftraggeber
Chrysalis Records
Record sleeve for Phillip
Goodhand-Tait's 'Teaching an
old dog new tricks'. Airbrush
and gouache, in colour.
Pochette pour le disque de
Phillip Goodhand-Tait 'Teaching
an old dog new tricks'
(Apprendre à un vieux singe
à faire la grimace). Aérographe
et gouache, en couleurs.
Plattenhülle für Phillip
Goodhand-Taits 'Teaching an
old dog new tricks' (Einem alten
Hund neue Tricks beibringen).
Gouache und Spritztechnik,
farbig.

Artist/Artiste/Künstler
Etienne Delessert
Art/Director/Directeur
Artistique
Etienne Delessert
Client/Auftraggeber
Disques Mary-Josée
Record cover illustration for
'Henri Dès chante pour les
enfants, Cache Cache', (Henri
Dès sings for children 'Hide
and Seek') nineteen songs
for children. Inks and pencils,
in colour.
Illustration pour pochette de
disque pour 'Henri Dès chante
pour les enfants, Cache Cache',
dix-neuf chansons pour
enfants. Encres et crayons, en
couleurs.
Illustration für eine Plattenhülle
für 'Henri Dès chante pour les
enfants, Cache Cache' (Henri
Dès singt für Kinder 'Versteck-
spiel'), neunzehn Kinderlieder.
Tusche und Farbstifte, farbig.

TROIS PETITS GARÇONS

LA FEUILLE ET L'ÉCUREUIL

LE GROS CHAT GOURMAND

MA PETITE SŒUR

UN MOINEAU SUR TON DOS

LES OURSONS LES REQUINS, LES KANGOUROUS ET LES OUISTITIS

L'ESCARGOT

LAPIN ALBINOS

LA BÊTE À BON DIEU

CACHE-CACHE

MON GROS LOUP MON P'TIT LOUP

LE FACTEUR

LA MÉLASSE

LES PETITS CANARDS

Artist/Artiste/Künstler
Jeff Cummins
Designer/Maquettiste/Gestalter
Jeff Cummins
Art Director/Directeur
Artistique
Aubrey Powell
Design Group/Groupe de
Graphistes/Design-Gruppe
Hipgnosis
Client/Auftraggeber
**McCartney Productions
Limited**
Record sleeve for the orchestral
version of Paul McCartney's
'Ram', arranged by Percy
Thrillington. Gouache.
Pochette de disque pour la
version orchestrée de 'Ram'
de Paul McCartney, arrangée
par Percy Thrillington.
Gouache.
Plattenhülle für die Orchester-
Version von Paul McCartneys
'Ram', arrangiert von Percy
Thrillington. Gouache.

Artist/Artiste/Künstler
Jeff Cummins
Art Director/Directeur
Artistique
Aubrey Powell
Design Group/Groupe de
Graphistes/Design-Gruppe
Hipgnosis
Client/Auftraggeber
**McCartney Productions
Limited**
Record sleeve for the album
'Wings over America', designed
to illustrate the colour and
excitement of a live Wings show.
Gouache.
Pochette pour l'album 'Wings
over America', créée pour
illustrer la couleur et l'agitation
d'un show des Wings. Gouache.
Plattenhülle für 'Wings over
America' (Wings in Amerika),
die die Buntheit und Aufregung
einer live Wings Veranstaltung
zeigen soll. Gouache.

Artist/Artiste/Künstler
Ri Kaiser
Art Director/Directeur
Artistique
Otto H Ruthenkolk
Client/Auftraggeber
Kellogg Deutschland GmbH
Design for Corn Flakes packet.
A life-size clown's mask,
designed to be cut out by
children. Airbrush and gouache.
Maquette pour une boite de Corn
Flakes. Masque de clown,
grandeur nature, destiné à être
découpé par les enfants.
Aérographe et gouache.
Design für eine Corn Flakes
Packung. Eine lebensgrosse
Clowns-Maske zum
Ausschneiden für Kinder.
Gouache und Spritztechnik.

Film
This section includes
film animation, television
advertising, television
programme titles or
credits and cinema
advertising.

Film
Cette section comprend
animation filmée,
publicité télévisée, titres
ou génériques de pro-
grammes de télévision
et publicité cinémato-
graphique.

Filme
Dieser Abschnitt umfasst
Trickfilme, Fernsehwer-
bung, Programm-Titel
oder Namensvorspann
und Werbung im Kino.

Artist/Artiste/Künstler
Jerry Hibbert
Animator/Dessinateur de Films
d'Animation/Trickfilmzeichner
Jerry Hibbert
Director/Réalisateur/Regisseur
Jerry Hibbert
Producer/Directeur/Produzent
Larry Sonneck
Editor/Monteur/Cutter
Ian Llande
Rostrum Camera/Caméra du
Rostre/Rostrum Kamera
Peter Turner
Production Company/
Compagnie de Productions/
Produktionsgesellschaft
TV Cartoons
Client/Auftraggeber
Municaps
20 second colour television
commercial for Municaps energy
tablets, entitled "Planks".
Spot publicitaire de 20 secondes
pour des cachets fortifiants
Municaps, intitulé "Planks."
20-Sekunden TV-Werbespot in
Farbe für Municaps Energie-
tabletten mit dem Titel "Planks"
(Planken).

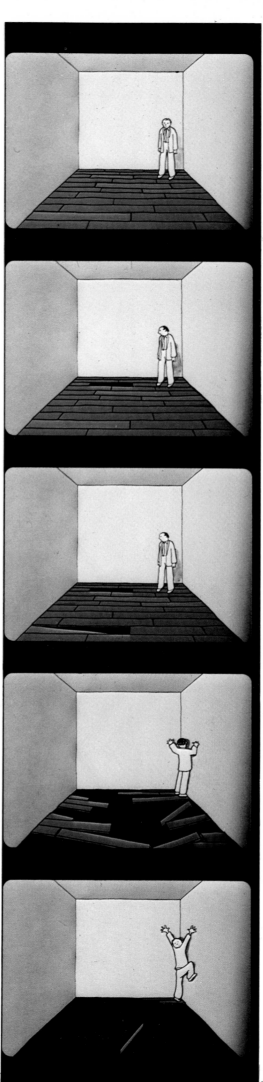

Artist/Artiste/Künstler
Russell Hall
Animator/Dessinateur de Films
d'Animation/Trickfilmzeichner
Russell Hall
Director/Réalisateur/Regisseur
Russell Hall
Art Director/Directeur
Artistique
John Hegarty
Producer/Directeur/Produzent
Judy Sheldon
Editor/Monteur/Cutter
Rod Howick
Advertising Agency/Agence de
Publicité/Werbeagentur
TBWA Limited
Production Company/
Compagnie de Productions/
Produktionsgesellschaft
Richard Williams Animation
Client/Auftraggeber
Johnson & Johnson Limited
Advertising Managers/Directeurs
de la Publicité/Werbeleiter
Todd Civardi
Denise Corbett
30 second colour television
commercial for Johnson &
Johnson cotton buds, "Button
Cods."
Spot publicitaire de 30 secondes
pour les cotons tiges Johnson &
Johnson, "Button Cods."
30-Sekunden TV-Werbespot in
Farbe für Johnson & Johnson
Wattestäbchen "Button Cods."

Artist/Artiste/Künstler
Georges Lemoine
Animator/Dessinateur de Films
d'Animation/Trickfilmzeichner
Georges Lemoine
Art Directors/Directeurs
Artistiques
Dominique Lacoste
Alain Pontecorvo
Copywriter/Rédacteur/Texter
Philippe Morlighem
Producer/Directeur/Produzent
Francis Bonduel
Advertising Agency/Agence de
Publicité/Werbeagentur
Roux Seguela Cayzac
et Goudard
Production Company/
Compagnie de Productions/
Produktionsgesellschaft
Manivelle
Client/Auftraggeber
Caisse Nationale de
Crédit Agricole
Advertising Managers/Directeurs
de la Publicité/Werbeleiter
Jean-Louis Caballé
Bruno Latappy
Television commercial for
Crédit Agricole.
Spot publicitaire pour le
Crédit Agricole.
TV-Werbespot für die
Crédit Agricole.

Artist/Artiste/Künstler
Richard Purdum
Animator/Dessinateur de Films
d'Animation/Trickfilmzeichner
Richard Purdum
Director/Réalisateur/Regisseur
Richard Purdum
Copywriter/Rédacteur/Texter
John Webster
Producer/Directeur/Produzent
Anne Tobin
Editor/Monteur/Cutter
Rod Howick
Advertising Agency/Agence de
Publicité/Werbeagentur
Boase Massimi Pollitt Univas
Partnership
Production Company/
Compagnie de Productions/
Produktionsgesellschaft
Richard Williams Animation
Client/Auftraggeber
Cadbury Schweppes Limited
Marketing Director/Directeur
du Marketing
Mike Handley
30 second colour television
commercial for Cresta, entitled
"Dance".
Spot publicitaire de 30 secondes
pour Cresta, intitulé "Dance"
(Danse).
30-Sekunden TV-Werbespot in
Farbe für Cresta mit dem Titel
"Dance" (Tanz).

Artist/Artiste/Künstler
Ray Jelliffe
Animator/Dessinateur de Films
d'Animation/Trickfilmzeichner
Richard Purdum
Copywriter/Rédacteur/Texter
Ray Jelliffe
Producer/Directeur/Produzent
Ray Jelliffe
Editor/Monteur/Cutter
Rod Howick
Advertising Agency/Agence de
Publicité/Werbeagentur
**Newlands Knight & Round
Limited**
Production Company/
Compagnie de Productions/
Produktionsgesellschaft
Richard Williams Animation
Client/Auftraggeber
Parke Davis & Company
Marketing Manager/Directeur
du Marketing
D O'Sullivan
15 second television commercial
for Benylets, "Olympic Torch
Runner".
Spot publicitaire de 15 secondes
pour Benylets, "Olympic Torch
Runner" (Coureur olympique
à flambeau).
15-Sekunden TV-Werbespot für
Benylets, "Olympic Torch
Runner" (Träger der olympischen
Flamme).

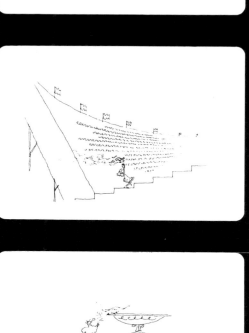

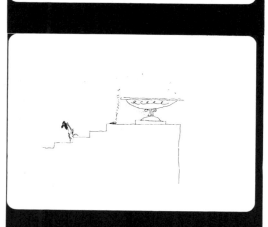

Artist/Artiste/Künstler
Tony White
Animator/Dessinateur de Films
d'Animation/Trickfilmzeichner
Tony White
Director/Réalisateur/Regisseur
Tony White
Copywriter/Rédacteur/Texter
Tony Evershed
Designer/Maquettiste/Gestalter
Ken Rinciari
Producer/Directeur/Produzent
Tony Evershed
Advertising Agency/Agence de
Publicité/Werbeagentur
The Creative Business
Production Company/
Compagnie de Productions/
Produktionsgesellschaft
Richard Williams Animation
Client/Auftraggeber
Guardian Newspapers
Marketing Director/Directeur
du Marketing
Gordon Thompson
60 second television commercial
for 'The Guardian' newspaper,
entitled "Odyssey".
Spot publicitaire de 60 secondes
pour le quotidien 'The Guardian',
intitulé "Odyssey".
60-Sekunden TV-Werbespot für
die Zeitung 'The Guardian'
mit dem Titel "Odyssey".

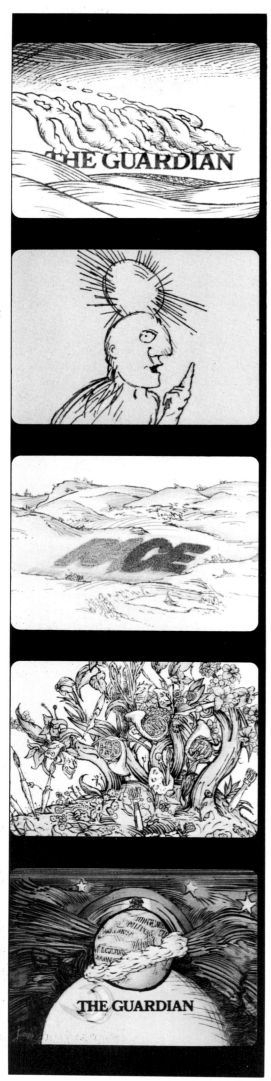

Artist/Artiste/Künstler
Peter Till
Animator/Dessinateur de Films
d'Animation/Trickfilmzeichner
Tony Payne
Cameraman/Caméra/Kamera
Rik Stratton
Director/Réalisateur/Regisseur
Tom Huish
Producer/Directeur/Produzent
Major Steadman
Production Company/
Compagnie de Productions/
Produktionsgesellschaft
Dragon Productions
Client/Auftraggeber
Geigy Pharmaceuticals
Promotional film for Geigy
Pharmaceuticals, showing
different phobias. Pen and ink,
in black and white.
Film pour la promotion de Geigy
Pharmaceuticals, montrant
différentes phobies. Plume
et encre, en noir et blanc.
Promotionsfilm für Geigy
Pharmaceuticals über
verschiedene Phobien.
Feder und Tusche, schwarzweiss.

Artist/Artiste/Künstler
Oscar Grillo
Animator/Dessinateur de Films
d'Animation/Trickfilmzeichner
Oscar Grillo
Director/Réalisateur/Regisseur
Oscar Grillo
Art Director/Directeur
Artistique
Peter Ibbitson
Copywriter/Rédacteur/Texter
David Brown
Producer/Directeur/Produzent
Linda Downes
Editor/Monteur/Cutter
Terry Brown
Rostrum Camera/Caméra du
Rostre/Rostrum Kamera
Richard Wolff
Advertising Agency/Agence de
Publicité/Werbeagentur
**Collett Dickenson Pearce &
Partners Limited**
Production Company/
Compagnie de Productions/
Produktionsgesellschaft
Dragon Productions
Client/Auftraggeber
EMI Records Limited
60 second television commercial,
"Frank Sinatra's Greatest Hits".
Spot publicitaire de 60 secondes,
"Frank Sinatra's Greatest Hits"
(Les plus grands succès de
Frank Sinatra).
60-Sekunden TV-Werbespot,
"Frank Sinatra's Greatest Hits"
(Frank Sinatras grösste Hits).

Artists/Artistes/Künstler
Bob Cosford
Tom Taylor
Animators/Dessinateurs de
Films d'Animation/Trickfilm-
zeichner
Bob Cosford
Tom Taylor
Designer/Maquettiste/Gestalter
Sid Sutton
Rostrum Camera/Caméra du
Rostre/Rostrum Kamera
Vic Cummings
Client/Auftraggeber
BBC Television
The opening titles for the
BBC television drama series
"Pennies From Heaven."
Premiers titres pour la série
dramatique de la télévision
BBC "Pennies From Heaven."
Vorspann für die BBC Fernseh-
serie "Pennies From Heaven"
(Pennies des Himmels).

Artist/Artiste/Künstler
Cynthia Pickard
Director/Réalisateur/Regisseur
Pauline Talbot
Animator/Dessinateur de Films
d'Animation/Trickfilmzeichner
Roy Jackson
Production Company/
Compagnie de Productions/
Produktionsgesellschaft
BBC Television
Graphic Design Department
Opening titles for "Jackanory,"
a children's television
programme.
Premiers titres pour "Jackanory",
programme de télévision pour
enfants.
Vorspann für "Jackanory," eine
Fernsehsendung für Kinder.

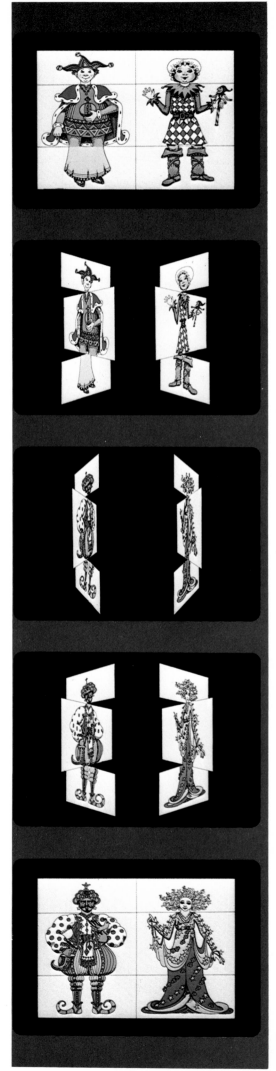

Artist/Artiste/Künstler
Martine Robin
Animator/Dessinateur de Films
d'Animation/Trickfilmzeichner
Martine Robin
Director/Réalisateur/Regisseur
Jean Caillon
Rostrum Cameraman/Caméra
du rostre/Rostrum Kamera
Gilles Delli-Zotti
Production Company/
Compagnie de Productions/
Produktionsgesellschaft
Films 33 SARL
"Les Dépressions."
(Depressionen).

Artist/Artiste/Künstler
Roland Topor
Animator/Dessinateur de Films
d'Animation/Trickfilmzeichner
Roland Topor
Director/Réalisateur/Regisseur
Michel Vadon
Copywriter/Rédacteur/Texter
Philippe Maraninchi
Producer/Directeur/Produzent
Francis Bonduel
Advertising Agency/Agence de
Publicité/Werbeagentur
**Roux Seguela Cayzac
et Goudard**
Production Company/
Compagnie de Productions/
Produktionsgesellschaft
Hamster
Client/Auftraggeber
Carrefour
Advertising Manager/Directeur
de la Publicité/Werbeleiter
Jacques Bordelais
Television commercial for
Carrefour, as yet not shown.
Spot publicitaire pour
Carrefour, pas encore montré.
TV-Werbespot für Carrefour,
bisher noch nicht gezeigt.

Unpublished
This section consists of
unpublished work.

Oeuvres Non Publiées
Cette section comprend
les oeuvres non publiées.

**Unveröffentlichte
Arbeiten**
Dieser Abschnitt umfasst
unveröffentlichte
Arbeiten.

Artist/Artiste/Künstler
Alwyn Clayden
College project. Silk screen,
hand separated four colour set.
Projet de college.
Sérigraphie, en quadrachrome.
College-Arbeit.
Siebdruck, handgezeichnete
Farbauszüge.

Artist/Artiste/Künstler
Pierre Peyrolle
"The Ghost of David Caspar
Friedrich". Oils.
"The Ghost of David Caspar
Friedrich" (Le Fantôme de
David Caspar Friedrich).
Huile.
"The Ghost of David Caspar
Friedrich" (Der Geist David
Caspar Friedrichs). Öl.

Artist/Artiste/Künstler
Anne Howeson
Reportage drawings, London,
Paris, Boston. Coloured
pencil, in colour.
Dessins de reportage, Londres,
Paris, Boston. Crayon de
couleur, en couleurs.
Reportage Zeichnungen –
London, Paris, Boston.
Farbstifte, farbig.

Artist/Artiste/Künstler
Giovanni Mulazzani
Acrylic on canvas.
Acrylique sur toile.
Acryl auf Leinwand.

Artist/Artiste/Künstler
Giovanni Mulazzani
Acrylic on canvas.
Acrylique sur toile.
Acryl auf Leinwand.

Artist/Artiste/Künstler
Boogie Corke
Water-colour and airbrush,
in colour.
Aquarelle et aérographe, en
couleurs.
Wasserfarben und Spritztechnik,
farbig

Artist/Artiste/Künstler
Chris Jones
"She", illustration for the book
by Rider Haggard. One of a
series of drawings following a
visit to Egypt by the artist, who
was awarded the Thames
Television Travel Bursary for
1977. Ink and coloured pencil,
in colour.
"She", illustration pour le livre
de Rider Haggard. L'un d'une
série de dessins exécutés après
un voyage en Egypte par l'artiste,
qui reçut la bourse de voyage
1977 de Thames Television.
Encre et crayon de couleur, en
couleurs.
"She" (Sie), Illustration für das
Buch von Rider Haggard,
innerhalb einer Serie von
Zeichnungen über eine Reise
des Künstlers nach Ägypten,
aufgrund des Thames Television
Reisestipendiums 1977.
Tusche und Farbstifte, farbig.

Artist/Artiste/Künstler
Philip Castle
"Gilda's Flypast".
Gouache.
"Gilda's Flypast" (Le défile
aérien de Gilda).
Gouache.
"Gilda's Flypast" (Gildas
Flugparade). Gouache.

Artist/Artiste/Künstler
Philip Castle
"A break in the traffic". Image used on poster for "Philip Castle" exhibition held at the Thumb Gallery, London, March 1978. Gouache, in colour.
"A break in the traffic." (Un trou dans la circulation). Image utilisée sur l'affiche de l'exposition "Philip Castle" à la Thumb Gallery, Londres, mars 1978. Gouache, en couleurs.
"A break in the traffic" (Eine Lücke im Verkehr). Image für ein Poster für die "Philip Castle" Ausstellung in der Thumb Gallerie, London, März 1978. Gouache, farbig.

251

Artist/Artiste/Künstler
Larry Learmonth
Oils on canvas, in colour.
Huile sur toile, en couleurs.
Öl auf Leinwand, farbig.

Artist/Artiste/Künstler
Larry Learmonth
Oils on canvas, in colour.
Huile sur toile, en couleurs.
Öl auf Leinwand, farbig.

Artist/Artiste/Künstler
Wolf Erlbruch
Oil over gouache on wood.
Huile par dessus gouache,
sur bois.
Öl über Gouache auf Holz.

Artist/Artiste/Künstler
Serge Fenech
Oils.
Huiles.
Öl.

Artist/Artiste/Künstler
Wolf Erlbruch
Oil over gouache on wood,
in colour.
Huile par dessus gouache
sur bois, en couleurs.
Öl über Gouache auf Holz,
farbig.

Artist/Artiste/Künstler
Michel Siméon
Oils, in colour.
Huile, en couleurs.
Öl, farbig.

Artist/Artiste/Künstler
Anne Howeson
"Mayfair Escorts".
Coloured pencils, in colour.
Crayons de couleur, en couleurs.
Farbstifte, farbig.

Artist/Artiste/Künstler
Anne Howeson
"Mayfair Escorts". Coloured
pencils, in colour.
Crayons de couleur, en couleurs.
Farbstifte, farbig.

Artist/Artiste/Künstler
Anne Howeson
"Mayfair Escorts". Coloured
pencils, in colour.
Crayons de couleur, en couleurs.
Farbstifte, farbig.

Artist/Artiste/Künstler
Robert Mason
"Adam and Eve". Water-colour,
gouache and inks, in colour.
"Adam and Eve". Aquarelle,
gouache et encres, en couleurs.
"Adam and Eve" (Adam und Eva).
Wasserfarben, Gouache und
Tusche, farbig.

ADAM & EVE.

Artist/Artiste/Künstler
Michael Pönnighaus
Water-colour, inks and airbrush, in colour.
Aquarelle, encres et aérographe, en couleurs.
Wasserfarben, Tusche und Spritztechnik, farbig.

Artist/Artiste/Künstler
Paul Slater
"Sabotaged", for a college
exhibition entitled "Hate."
Acrylic, in colour.
"Sabotaged" (Saboté), pour une
exposition de college, intitulée
"Hate" (La Haine).
Acrylique, en couleurs.
"Sabotaged" (Sabotiert), für
eine College Ausstellung
zum Thema "Hate" (Hass).
Acryl, farbig.

Artists Addresses
Adresses des Artistes
Adressen der Künstler

Tom Adams, 133
Marden Hill, Hertford,
SG14 2NE, England.
Julian Allen, 41, 42, 43
31 Walker Street, New York,
NY 10013, USA.
Wayne Anderson, 168
16 Pagett Street, Kibworth
Beauchamp, Leicester, England.
Marshal Arisman, 59
314 West 100 Street, New York,
NY 10025, USA.
Alan Baker, 198
C/O The Zip Art Company,
Publishing House,
48 Grafton Way, London W1,
England.
Peter Barrett, 107
Madford House, Hemyock,
Cullompton, Devon, England.
Derek Benee, 166
Magic Box Studios, 21 New Row,
London WC2, England.
Guy Billout, 30, 85, 180, 200
222 West 15 Street, New York,
NY 10011, USA.
Stuart Bodek, 196
C/O Artist Partners,
14-18 Ham Yard, London W1.
England.
Fernando Botero, 118, 119
5 Boulevard du Palais,
75004 Paris, France.
Joelle Boucher, 122
99 Elysée 2, 78170 La Celle Saint
Cloud, France.
Marc Boxer, 120
34 Holland Villas Road,
London W14, England.
Glynn Boyd Harte, 185
28 Cloudesly Square,
London N1, England.
Peter Brookes, 26, 98, 99, 100,
146, 226
30 Vanbrugh Hill,
London SE3 7UF, England.
Christian Broutin, 174
13 Clos des Fosses Rouges,
Villeneuve Le Comte, 77, France.
Mick Brownfield, 84, 197
41 The Vineyard, Richmond,
Surrey.
Béat Brüsch, 264
Bossons 51, CH 1018 Lausanne,
Switzerland.
Pier Canosa, 137
Via Bari 33/57, Genoa, Italy.
Philip Castle, 54, 250, 251
56 Burnfoot Avenue,
London SW6, England.
Philippe Caron, 175
32 rue Henri Barbuss,
75005 Paris, France.
Hector Cattolica, 190
104 Boulevard Diderot,
75012 Paris, France.
Chloe Cheese, 92, 93, 218, 219
118 Leander Road, London SW2,
England.
Seymour Chwast, 202, 203
Push Pin Studios,
207 East 32 Street,
New York, USA.
Alwyn Clayden, 242
48 Portland Place, London W1,
England.
Marina Clement, 158
85 rue du Moulin des Près,
75013 Paris, France.
Alan Cober, 22, 23
95 Crotondan Road, Ossening,
New York, NY 10562, USA.
Sue Coe, 18, 36, 37, 86
Apartment 3C, 214 East 84 Street.
New York, USA.
Roy Coombs, 70
3 St. Thomas Park, Lymington,
Hampshire, England.
Boogie Corke, 248
6 Garrick Street, London WC2,
England.
Bob Cosford, 238
10 Barleymow Passage,
London W4 4PH, England.
Barry Craddock, 169
6 Shardeloes Road,
London SE14, England.
Jan Cremer, 63
Singel 237, Amsterdam,
Holland.

Jeff Cummins, 230
74 Crib Street, Ware,
Hertfordshire, SG12 9HG,
England.
Graham Dean, 53
C/O Nicholas Treadwell Gallery,
36 Chiltern Street, London W1,
England.
Herman Degkwitz, 80, 81
2201 Hohenfelde über Elmshorn,
Holstein, West Germany.
Etienne Delessert, 57, 128, 202,
203, 229
Domaine du Bochet,
1025 St. Sulpice, Switzerland.
Christian Desbois, 222
Chateau du Parc,
78430 Louveciennes, France.
Michel Dubré, 164
12 rue St. Catherine,
La Varenne St. Hilaire,
9014 France.
Wolf Erlbruch, 254, 256
Holthauserstrasse 150,
56 Wuppertal 21, Nordrrheim,
Westfalen, West Germany.
Jean Luc Falque, 163, 186
41 rue de l'Eglise, 75015 Paris,
France.
Serge Fenech, 255
02 rue Ordener, 75008 Paris,
France.
Claude Ferrand, 265
42 rue Cronstadt, 75015 Paris,
France.
Peter Fischer, 74, 75, 76, 77
Winkeldorf Nr. 8,
2134 Horstedt, West Germany.
Alan Fisher, 213
C/O CGA, Onslow House,
60-66 Saffron Hill, London EC1,
England.
Peter Fluck, 38, 39, 40
Victoria House, Victoria Street,
Cambridge, England.
Alain Le Foll, 202, 203
2 rue Jules Chapelain, 75006
Paris, France.
André François, 73, 202, 203
Grisy Les Platres, 95810, France.
Rainer Cornelius Friz, 111
Mendelssohnstrasse 5A,
8000 Munich 60, West Germany.
Brian Froud, 61, 68
C/O Artist Partners,
14-18 Ham Yard, London W1,
England.
Henri Galeron,
45 rue Racine, 92120 Montrouge,
France.
Jooce Garrett, 159
C/O Artist Partners,
14-18 Ham Yard, London W1,
England.
Kees van Gelder, 55
Rokin 111, Amsterdam, Holland.
Adrian George, 94, 95, 127
55 Linden Gardens, London W2,
England.
Guy Gladwell, 167
20 Harley Road, London NW3,
England.
Milton Glaser, 19, 191, 202, 203
Milton Glaser Incorporated,
755 Second Avenue, New York,
NY 10017, USA.
Alex Gnidziejko, 58
37 Alexander Avenue, Madison,
New Jersey, USA.
Josse Goffin, 88
12 rue Th. Decock,
Bossut Gottechain 5989,
Belgium.
Mike Golding, 178, 179
Top Drawers, Lijnbaansgracht
162, Amsterdam, Holland.
Erhard Göttlicher, 51, 124, 125
Neuweg 5, D-2082 Uetersen bei
Hamburg, West Germany.
Oscar Grillo, 237
59 The Ridgeway, London W3,
England.
Brian Grimwood, 201
Hat Studio, 36 Wellington Street,
London WC2, England.
Russell Hall, 234
C/O Richard Williams
Animation, 13 Soho Square,
London W1, England.
Harry Hants, 154
C/O Artist Partners,
14-18 Ham Yard, London W1,
England.

George Hardie, 140, 141
NTA Studios, 44 Earlham Street,
London WC2, England.
Robin Harris, 44, 52, 126
60 Weltje Road,
London W6 9LT, England.
Hergé, 181
Editions Le Lombard,
2-11 Avenue Ph Spaak,
Brussels, Belgium.
Jean Olivier Héron,
La Garderie du Bonjour
Ker Pissot, 858350 Ille d'Yeu,
France.
Jerry Hibbert, 234
TV Cartoons Limited,
70 Charlotte Street, London W1,
England.
Marie Hofmann, 55
Brugmanstraat 55, Eindhoven,
Holland.
Werner Hofmann, 28
Gesegnetmattstrasse 1,
CH 6000 Lucerne, Switzerland.
Heiner H Hoier, 145
Lange Reihe 84, 2 Hamburg 1,
West Gemany.
Anne Howeson, 143, 244, 245,
258, 259, 260
91 Cloudesley Road, London N1,
England.
John Ireland,
C/O The Valerie Kemp Agency,
28 Bramham Gardens,
London SW5, England.
Ray Jelliffe, 236
Newlands Knight & Round
Limited, 33 Bruton Street,
London W1, England.
Chris Jones, 249
11 Effingham Road,
Long Ditton, Surrey, England.
Ri Kaiser, 231
Frohmestrasse 126,
D 2000 Hamburg 61,
West Germany.
Keleck, 150
28 rue Didot, 75004 Paris,
France.
Lionel Koechlin, 29, 82, 83
6 rue Edmond About,
75016 Paris, France.
Peter Knock, 35, 66
52 Westbourne Grove,
Westcliff on Sea, Essex,
England.
Andrzej Krauze, 121
Anieli Krzywon 2 m 155,
01 391 Warsaw, Poland.
H P Kunkel, 206, 207
Hasenhohe 5, 2000 Hamburg 55,
West Germany.
Claude Lapointe, 136, 151
1 rue de Bâle, Geisposheim,
67400 Illkirch, Graffenstaden,
France.
Roger Law, 38, 39, 40
Victoria House, Victoria Street,
Cambridge, England.
Larry Learmonth, 71, 199,
252, 253
Telephone:
Studio 10, London, England.
01-323 1544
Radlett Hertfordshire, England.
Radlett 6048.
Alan Lee,
C/O Artist Partners, 132
14-18 Ham Yard, London W1,
England.
Paul Leith, 187
37 Therapia Road,
London SE22, England.
Martin Leman, 91
28 Ripplevale Grove,
London N1, England.
Georges Lemoine, 138, 139,
235
Le Chataigner, La Haye,
76780 Argueil, France.
Pierre Le-Tan, 90, 102, 103, 224
26 rue Singer, 75016 Paris,
France.
Tom Liddell, 212
192 Forest Drive, South Park,
Lytham, Lancashire, England.
Barbara Lofthouse, 110
Allen House, 88 Whitton Road,
Hounslow TW3 2DF, England.
Michael Lunt, 221
9 Laurel Hill, Dun Laoghaire,
County Dublin, Eire.

Jean Claude Lutton, 227
9 rue Tiphaine, 75015 Paris,
France.
Gerlinde Mader, 215
Brabanterstrasse 16,
8 Munich 40, West Germany.
Kevin W Maddison, 123
C/O Ash & Grant,
120B Pentonville Road,
London N1 9JB, England.
Robert Mason, 96, 261
91 Cloudesly Road,
London N1 0EL, England.
Tony Meeuwissen, 147
Telephone: Basingstoke,
England, 0256 61051.
Sara Midda, 217
19 Steeles Road, London NW3,
England.
Russell Mills, 97, 104
22 Torriano Cottages,
London NW5, England.
Jan Mlodozeniec, 204, 205
Ul Naruszewicza 3 m 7,
02627 Warsaw, Poland.
Donna Muir, 148, 149
NTA Studios, 44 Earlham Street,
London WC2, England.
Giovanni Mulazzani, 246, 247
Via A Lecchi 7, Milan, Italy.
Alex Murawski, 34
Room 3410 A, 600 North
McClurg Court, Chicago,
Illinois, 60611, USA.
Lawrence Mynott, 45
41 The Vineyard, Richmond,
Surrey, England.
Keith McEwan, 188
Top Drawers, Lijnbaansgracht
162, Amsterdam, Holland.
Mike Noomé, 228
C/O Andrew Archer Associates,
10 Glentworth Street,
London NW1, England.
Mariet Numan, 79
Anjelierstraat 92, Amsterdam,
Holland.
Jean Palayer, 142
La Chartronnière,
26190 St. Thomas en Royans,
Drome, France.
Gabriel Pascalini, 189
21 rue de l'Eglise,
Le Coudray Montceaux,
91830 Essones, France.
Neil Patterson, 156
Wawcott House,
The Wilderness, Elcot Turn,
Near Kintbury, Newbury,
Berkshire, England.
Pierre Peyrolle, 223, 243
C/O European Illustration,
12 Carlton House Terrace,
London SW1Y 5AH, England.
Cynthia Pickard, 238
42 Tasso Road, London W6,
England.
Christian Piper, 31
487 Broadway, Room 1201,
New York, NY 10013, USA.
Gillian Platt, 106
Garden Studio, 11 Broad Court,
London WC2, England.
Monica Polasz, 101, 105
Winsener Strasse 11,
21 Hamburg 90, West Germany.
Ian Pollock, 129, 144
7 Grove Terrace, Highgate Road,
London NW5, England.
Michel Ponnighaus, 262
Redderblock 31, 2 Hamburg 73,
West Germany.
Richard Purdum, 235
C/O Richard Williams
Animation, 13 Soho Square,
London W1, England.
René van Raalte, 211
Tiber 6, Amstelveen, Holland.
Jean Marie Renard, 225
27 rue de Flers, 75015 Paris,
France.
Jean Michel Renault, 56
24 Boulevard Gambetta,
62100 Calais, France.
Willi Rieser, 172, 173
Angwieler Strasse 69,
8302 Kloten Augwiel,
Switzerland.
Martine Robin, 239
1 rue Joseph Bara, 75006 Paris,
France.
Arthur Robins, 60, 193, 194
30 Neal Street, London WC2,
England.

Joost Roelofsz, 108, 109
Oude Schaus 6, Amsterdam,
Holland.
Marina Langer-Rosa, 195
Droste-Hulshoff Strasse 15,
D 5000 Cologne 51,
West Germany.
Helmut Rottke, 184
Dominikanderstrasse 79,
4000 Dusseldorf, West Germany.
Will Rowlands, 170, 171
40 Temple Road, Sale, Cheshire,
M33 2FP, England.
Paul Sample, 69, 165
Old Vicarage, Ash Magna,
Near Whitchurch, Salop,
England.
Arnold Schwartzman, 160, 161
Saul Bass & Associates,
7039 Sunset Boulevard,
Los Angeles, California 90028,
USA.
Michel Siméon, 257
163 rue du Charenton,
75012 Paris, France.
Paul Slater, 263
81 Stanhope Avenue,
London N3, England.
Ralph Steadman, 20, 21, 32,
33, 46, 47, 48, 49, 87, 134, 135
C/O European Illustration,
12 Carlton House Terrace,
London SW1, England.
Nick Taggart, 50, 64, 65, 67
2643 Crestmore Place,
Los Angeles, California 90065,
USA.
Jacques Tardi, 192
C/O Editions Castermann,
66 rue Bonaparte, 75006 Paris,
France.
Tom Taylor, 238
34 Great Livermere, Suffolk,
England.
A Ramon Gonzalez Teja, 72
Ruiz Perello, 13 Madrid 28,
Spain.
Eric Tenney, 89
C/O Artist Partners,
14-18 Ham Yard, London W1.
Andre Thijssen, 130, 131
Kempering 717, 1104 KE
Amsterdam zuidoost, Holland.
Guenther Thumer, 27
Hohenzollernstrasse 16,
8000 Munich 16, West Germany.
Peter Till, 237
42 Berkeley Road, London N8,
England.
Titus, 162
35 rue Savier, 92240 Malakoff,
France.
Roland Topor, 114, 115, 116, 117,
239
47 rue de Boulainvilliers,
75016 Paris, France.
Barry Trengrove, 182, 183
92A St. Johns Wood High Street,
London NW8, England.
Erno Tromp, 62
Keizersgracht 584, Amsterdam,
Holland.
Peter Le Vasseur, 24, 25
Coin des Arquets,
Rue de Catillion, St. Peters,
Guernsey, Channel Islands.
John Verberk, 214
Comeniusstraat 491,
1065 BX Amsterdam, Holland.
Manfred Vogel, 78
Wigstrasse 9, 43 Essen 16,
West Germany.
Dorothee Walter, 155
Fullstrasse 7, 8 Munich 90,
West Germany.
Martin White, 216
1 St. Mary's Cottages,
Longworth, Abingdon,
Oxon OX13 5HG, England.
Tony White, 236
C/O Richard Williams
Animation, 13 Soho Square,
London W1, England.
Bruno K Wiese, 210
Allhornweg 7, 2000 Hamburg 67,
West Germany.
Bob Wilson, 157
The Art Directors Studio &
Partners Limited,
11 Osborne Mansions,
Luxborough Street, London W1,
England.

Past contributors whose work has already featured in European Illustration, who can be contacted through our office, are as follows:

Les artistes, dont le travail a déjà paru dans European Illustration, dont les adresses sont disponibles de notre bureau, sont les suivants:

Illustratoren, deren Arbeiten in vergangenen Jahren in European Illustration erschienen sind und die durch unser Büro erreichbar sind:

Stephen Adams
Gillian Adsett
Anita Albus
John Alcorn
Alan Aldridge
John Allin
Andrew Aloof
Hal Ambro
Kjell Ivan Anderson
Apicella
Areopage
Jean Marie Assenet
Babs
Sydney Badmin
Claude Bailleul
Richard Baldwin
Norman Barber
Arthur Barbosa
Henry Barnett
Alberte Barsacq
Saul Bass
John Bauer
David Baxter
Nicola Bayley
Pete Beard
Ian Beck
Anthon Beeke
Wolfgang Bellingradt
Madeleine Bennet
M J Bennallack Hart
Peter Bentley
Arja van der Berg
Torsten Bergentz
Jean Louis Besson
Liz Bijl
Jacques Billebeau
Carol Binch
Paul Birbeck
Malcolm Bird
Peter Blake
Quentin Blake
Robert Blagden
Karin Blume
Keith Bonen
Bernard Bonhomme
René Botti
Pierre Bouille
Roger Bourne
Leonora Box
Bob Brett
Tom Brooks
David Bryant
Roman Buj
David Bull
Bill Butt
Patricia Caley
Alastair Campbell
Roy Carruthers
Giovanni Caselli
Tony Cattaneo
Olivier Cauquil
Leslie Chapman
Henri Chauvin
Adrian Chesterman
Graham Clarke
John Clark
Nicole Claveloux
Roger Coleman
Chris Collicott
Terry Collins
Michel Comte
Robert Comte
Max Condula
Peter Cook
Ken Cox
Patrick Cox
Alan Cracknell
Brian Craker
Mick Crane
Jon Cramer
Gino D'Achille
Salvador Dali
Rosalind Dallas

Terence Dalley
Pierre Paul Darigo
Claire Davies
David Davies
Keith Davis
Paul Davis
Richard Dearing
Carlo Demand
Mike Dempsey
Gérard Deshayes
Serge Clément Despres
Phil Dobson
Pierre Ducordeau
Andrzej Dudzinski
Jean Louis Dufour
Gert Dumbar
Bernard Durin
Jennifer Eachus
Anthony Earnshaw
Heinz Edelmann
Yrjö Edelmann
Jeffery Edwards
Robert Ellis
Pauline Ellison
Roy Ellsworth
David English
Malcolm English
Michael English
Gil Evans
Frans Evenhuis
Gerald Eveno
John Farman
Michael Farrell
Beatrice Fassell
Patricia Faulkner
Christine Fenech
Dan Fern
Guy Fery
Philippe Fix
Alan Fletcher
Jean Michel Folon
David Forbes
Michael Foreman
M Forgas
Nancy Fouts
Malcolm Fowler
Francès
François Frances
David Frankland
Harriet Freedman
David Freeman
Michael Gabriel
Gallardo
Gangloff
Pat Gavin
Gaudriault
Harry Geelen
William Geldart
Ginger Gibbons
John Gibbs
Tony Gibbs
Anne Yvonne Gilbert
Girodroux
Bernard Giroudroux
John Glashan
Derek Goldsmith
Bengt Good
Rick Goodale
John Gorham
Jean Paul Goude
Julian Graddon
Alastair Graham
Sophie Grandval
Giovanni Grasso
Lyn Gray
Leslie Greenwood
Robert Grossman
René Gruau
Walter Gudel
Jean Paul Guiems
Jean Pierre Guillemot
David Hancock
Hargrave Hands
Ken Harris
Malcolm Harrison
Richard Hess
Christopher Hill
Hans Hillman
Gillian Hills
Arno Hinz
Godi Hofmann
Paul Hogarth
David Hockney
Lars Hokanson
Bush Hollyhead
John Holmes
Nigel Holmes
Alun Hood
Robert Hook
Pierre Houles
Jannat Houston
Su Huntley
John Hurford

Peter Hutton
Vera Ibbett
David Jackson
Faith Jacques
Brian James
Werner Jeker
Michael Johnson
Allan Jones
Dan Jonsson
Jerry Joyner
David Juniper
Loris Kalasat
Pete Kelley
Peter Kelley
György Kemény
Ron Kirby
Traudy Klemm
Lawrence Klonaris
Edda Kochl
M Koether
Brian Knight
Royston Knipe
Ray Kyte
J Lacroix
Jean Laguarrigue
Ken Laidlaw
Peter Lampert
Urs Landis
Frank Langford
Jean Jacques Larrière
Patrice Larue
Sally Launder
John Lawrence
Bob Lawrie
Michael Leconte
Michael Leonard
Alain Leray
Jean Lessenich
Abe Levitow
Richard Lewis
Kenneth Lilly
Katrin Lindley
Michael Litherland
Ernst Litter
Bernard Lodge
Catherine Loeb
Antonio Lopez
M Loris
Lucques
John Mac
Muriel Mackenzie
Stewart Mackinnon
Euphemia Mactavish
Warren Madill
Hélène Majéra
Allan Manham
Richard Manning
Graham Marsh
James Marsh
Grzegorz Marszalek
Pauline Martin
Mina Martinez
Michael Mau
Fernando Maza
Ann Meisel
Lars Melander
Maupéou Merre
Pino Milas
Roland Millet
Glen Mitchell
Anthony Moore
Chris Moore
Norman Moore
Claude Morchoisne
Jonathan de Morgan
Morillon
Jean Mulatier
Bob Murdoch
Yves Musnier
Neil McDonald
Mike McInnery
Sean McMillan
James McMullan
Tony McSweeny
Navarres
George Nicholas
Peter North
Bengt Nystrom
Maximillien Odello
Ray Ogden
OPS
Barry O'Riordan
Richard Orr
Lucinda Osmond
Anders Österlin
Peter Owen
Patrick Oxenham
Helen Oxenbury
Françoise Pages
Jacques Parnel
Terry Pastor
David Pearce
David Penny

Graham Percy
Jean Maxim Perramon
Chantal Petit
Antonio Pimentel
Tom Piper
Laurent Pizzoti
Philippe Plaquin
David Pocknell
Philippe Poncet de la Grave
Gerry Preston
Nick Price
Anna Pugh
Michael Quarez
QED
Hans Georg Rauch
Charles Raymond
Paul Rayne
Alan Rees
Berselli Remo
Patrice Ricord
Jean Edouard Robert
Christine Robins
John Rose
Kristin Rosenberg
M Rosenthal
Anthony Ross
Rozier
Ken Rush
George Russell
Brian Sanders
Bill Sanderson
Sanseau
Claude Sardet
Gerald Scarfe
Renate Schlohmann
Binette Schroeder
Ronald Searle
Manfried Seelow
Roger Selden
Sylvie Selig
Ken Sequin
Faith Shannon
George Sharp
Shirtsleeve Studio
Yves Simard
Enrico Sio
Gerard Skögberg
Romain Slocombe
Andrew Smee
Anne Smith
Caroline Smith
Ken Smith
Trevor Smith
Heinz Spohr
Grzegorz Stańczyk
Birgitta Steen
Swip Stolk
Anne Strugnell
Brian Stymest
Simms Taback
Don Tait
Mike Terry
Ivan Theimer
John Thirsk
Graham Thompson
Jenny Thorne
Graham Thos
Yves Thos
Jacques Tosetto
Tessa Traeger
Michael Trevithick
John Tribe
Jan Peter Tripp
Guire Vaka
Celestino Valenti
Ans Vanemden
Claude Varieras
Pierre Varlet
Cyril Vassiliev
Cecil Vieweg
Friedrich Karl Waechter
Peter Wandrey
Peter Wane
Warwickshire Illustrators
Donald Watson
Norman Weaver
Peter Weever
Dietmar Wefers
Karin Welponer
Jeker Werner
Beatrix Wetter
Kay Wiedemann
John Wilkinson
Richard Williams
Chrissy Wilson
Franklin Wilson
John Wilson
Roland Wilson
Ray Winder
Ann Winterbotham
Charles White
Owen Wood
Sidney Wood

Janet Woolley
Chris Woolmer
Geoff Woolston
David Worth
Friere Wright
Joseph Wright
Tony Wright
Peter Wyss
Sato Yamamoto